# American Medical Association
Physicians dedicated to the health of America

# The
# Physician's
# Resume and
# Cover Letter
# Workbook

# The Physician's Resume and Cover Letter Workbook

Additional copies of this book (Product Number OP 206497) may be ordered by calling toll free 800 621-8335.

Internet address: http://www.ama-assn.org

ISBN 0-89970-888-9

Information contained in this publication does not constitute legal or business advice and should not be substituted for the independent advice of an attorney or business consultant. Opinions expressed in this publication are not necessarily those of the AMA.

BP37:97-346:3M:2/98

# Acknowledgments

The following people made significant contributions to the publication of this book. Their efforts are both acknowledged and appreciated.

## Author

Sharon L. Yenney, who developed the content and wrote the manuscript for the book, is Senior Vice President and Partner at CBY Associates, Inc. Formerly with Parkside Medical Services Corporation and the American Hospital Association, in her 14 years with CBY Ms. Yenney has consulted with businesses, institutions, professional associations, and public and private agencies on a variety of health-related issues. She has drawn upon her organization development and teaching skills to assist both companies and medical practices in resolving business and personnel problems. For the American Medical Association, Ms. Yenney developed and presented a workshop of managed care for physicians—"Medicine in Transition: Strategies for Change"—to help them cope with changes in the health care marketplace.

Ms. Yenney is a widely published writer in the health care field, having authored publications for the American Psychological Association and the Washington Business Group on Health, among others. She holds a BFA from the University of New Mexico and an MS in Human Resource Development from George Washington University.

## Reviewers

Janice Robertson
Policy Analyst
Department of Young Physician Services
American Medical Association

Carol Sprague
Senior Corporate Recruiter
Division of Employee Relations and Placement
American Medical Association

## AMA Staff

Suzanne Fraker
Product Line Development Director
Product Line Development
American Medical Association

Jean Roberts
Senior Editor
Product Line Development
American Medical Association

J. D. Kinney
Marketing Manager
Marketing and Sales
American Medical Association

Selby Toporek
Senior Communications Coordinator
Marketing Services
American Medical Association

Special thanks to Pat Dragisic, Managing Editor, AMA Trade
Publishing, American Medical Association, who wrote the
Bibliography.

# Contents

# Introduction

This book is designed specifically for physicians who are preparing for a job search. Some of you may be seeking your first job; others, a professional change or a return to work after a hiatus. Still others of you may have had your career disrupted by the rapidly changing health care environment and ever-increasing competition for scarce practice opportunities. In short, you need a resume.

Many physicians prepare both a *curriculum vitae (CV)* and a *resume,* using each as appropriate. While the terms are sometimes used synonymously, the CV and resume are distinct documents used in different job search situations. Each document contains the same basic information, but the presentation of that information in terms of both detail and emphasis differs.

A curriculum vitae is the document of choice if you are applying for an academic position or some government positions. A lengthier document than the typical resume, the CV contains carefully detailed information about your qualifications and experience, including all academic honors, publications, and presentations given. The goal is to present to a prospective employer the breadth and depth of your accomplishments in the format that employer is accustomed to seeing.

A resume is appropriate for all other job search situations, especially if you are making a career change. In this case, you want to focus on the transferable skills you have gained from your past experience to emphasize how they qualify you for the job for which you are applying. In this book, we focus on preparing a resume in a chronological, functional, or combination format.

Regardless of the format used, the goal is to present a brief biological sketch of you as a job candidate, a review of your experience and work history, and other information that will help you make a good first impression on a prospective employer. Resumes go beyond the static, past-oriented work history that you have prepared over the years to meet credentialing requirements or complete the application process to obtain hospital privileges. Resumes and CVs are job-oriented documents designed to get the attention of a potential employer.

You do not need to revise your resume every time you apply for a job. Cover letters tailored to specific jobs will do that for you. While a great resume and a carefully crafted cover letter alone will not win a job for you, they may determine whether or not you get an interview so that you can demonstrate your abilities in person. A poorly prepared resume or poorly written cover letter may eliminate you from the interview pool.

This book considers the special concerns of physicians when writing their resumes:

- Demonstrating uniqueness among candidates who have similar educational backgrounds.

- Describing the practice of medicine in terms that recruiters and employers understand and delineating responsibilities and accomplishments.

- Showing how competencies gained in the practice of medicine can be applied to other types of employment.

- Sifting through work histories, continuing education courses, and non-medical experiences to highlight the important characteristics that provide an edge in the competition for jobs.

In the text of this book and through numerous samples and examples, these concerns are addressed and practical suggestions are offered.

*The Physician's Resume and Cover Letter Workbook* coaches you as you build your resume, proposes how you might use the document in seeking a job, suggests appropriate cover letters to help employers see how your experience fits with their job, and provides many practical checklists, samples, and writing examples. Skim through the chapters to discover those elements that you most need to liven up the description of your work history and experience. Then return to the recommendations and tips in each section to draft a resume that represents the best of your work life. Try your hand at writing unique cover letters for each job for which you apply. The checklists, samples, and other reminders in this book will help you review your work before you submit your personal documents to an employer.

Writing an effective resume, preparing good cover letters, and developing other materials to support your job search will take time. The piece that takes the most writing time initially is the resume, which fortunately doesn't need to be redone every time you apply for a job. Keep in mind that a well-prepared resume may result in a step forward in your career and is therefore well worth the time spent preparing it. Good luck.

# Chapter One

# Resumes

## Why you need a resume

Why prepare a resume? The simplest answer to this question is that your resume will help you get the job you want. But that response is too simple. A more complete answer includes the following reasons for writing a resume.

- A good resume presents your background completely and in the best light without your having to do so in person. Many adults are reluctant to highlight their accomplishments and achievements. Physicians, in particular, find their chosen field of medicine to be an interesting and rewarding career that is not always easy to articulate to laypeople. Describing to others what doctors experience or accomplish on a day-to-day basis is challenging. Preparing a full resume of your work and life experiences may be a struggle, but it is a good way to list all your contributions without feeling that you are boasting.

- A resume helps recruiters or interviewers focus on your strong points. By presenting your education, work experience, and other contributions in a logical, easy-to-understand format, you can lead recruiters to view your candidacy favorably even before an interview is scheduled.

- A good resume helps you pass initial screening processes that may be conducted by someone other than a professional interviewer/recruiter. Your application and resume may be screened for specific educational requirements or number of years of experience. You may wish to add your resume to the application forms required by some employers to ensure that all the information needed to pass the screening is available.

- A resume accompanied by a job-specific cover letter gives you an opportunity to state how your experience is well suited to the available job. It can help structure the *first* interview by giving the interviewer positive leads to explore—leads that you have created to highlight your unique qualities.

- A good resume may mean the difference between getting and not getting that first interview. A recruiter who is overwhelmed by dozens of resumes is likely to select only those that are well presented in order to reduce the number of candidates that must be reviewed.

- A factual, attractive, and well-organized resume establishes you as a professional with high standards and excellent writing skills— a plus on any job.

- Your resume stays with the recruiter once the interview is completed. It captures your strong points in writing and leaves a lasting impression.

- Writing a resume and cover letters forces you to focus on your accomplishments and your potential as a job candidate. Don't treat your resume as documentation of history. Do consider it a personal statement about yourself that you would like an employer to consider. A resume is for the future.

## What is included in a resume

Think of yourself as a product that you need to sell. Your resume is the sales brochure that contains a description of the product, identifies why it is better than other products that are available, and makes the reader want to find out more about the product. While is it difficult for professionals to accept that personal sales documents are needed, the paucity of jobs in medicine indicates that each of us needs to consider how best to present ourselves as a job candidate. In addition to the resume that "sells" you, the cover letters that you write will help you demonstrate how well your qualifications match the job that is available.

## Elements of a resume

The elements of a resume are simple. (But that doesn't make them easy to write!) Here is a list of the elements. Those marked with an asterisk denote elements that need to be included in every physician's resume; the unmarked ones are optional.

Heading*
Job objective
Education*
Highlights/skills/accomplishments
Work history*
Personal interests or activities*
Licenses, certifications, and
    appointments*
References

Other considerations:
    Honors or awards
    Professional societies
    Committees
    Research interests
    Publications, editorships,
      presentations
    Special skills
    Special training/continuing
      education
    Leadership positions

How to write and format each of these resume elements and how to handle unique circumstances are covered in Chapter Two.

Several items that once were traditional parts of a resume are not listed above and *should not be included.*

- *Personal information.* A potential employer is prohibited from asking for personal and family information, and you should not supply it on your resume. If there are overriding personal considerations that affect your candidacy, explain them in the cover letter or in an interview.

- *Salary history or requirements.* Even if you know what compensation you must have, don't list it on the resume. If the advertisement for a job asks specifically for salary history or requirements, indicate in your cover letter that salary requirements are negotiable depending on the responsibilities of the job and on compensation other than salary. If absolutely forced to give a salary history, put it in the cover letter and not on the resume. That way you won't have to delete that information the next time you want to send a resume.

- *Photographs.* These fall into the same category as personal information and should be avoided. (Unless you are applying for a modeling job!)

- *Nationality.* This is another personal information category that should not be listed except under special circumstances. If it is obvious from your education and work history that the United States is not your original home country, you may want to list your citizenship status. For example, you might say "Dual German/American citizenship with permanent residence in the US."

## Resume styles

To determine what style you should choose for your resume, consider both the information that you have to offer (ie, a lengthy work history or education only) and the type of job you are seeking (ie, continuing in the same field or making a career change). Choose from one of three basic styles: chronological, functional, or combination chronological/functional.

**Chronological.** The chronological style of resume, which is the most traditional, highlights experience, skills, and employment history in a single section; jobs are listed in reverse order beginning with the most recent (or current). Education may be listed chronologically or with the highest degree first.

### Tip

Regardless of the style you choose, prepare a chronological resume first in order to capture all your work and volunteer experiences. You can use this information as a chronological resume or to help you decide whether to arrange it in a different style.

The chronological style resume works best for individuals who have:

- Held a number of positions that show progress from lesser to higher degrees of responsibility.
- Filled a number of different positions, each of which requires an explanation or description.
- Demonstrated a stable employment pattern.

**Functional.** A functional style resume begins with a list of skills acquired through education and experience. The focus of the resume is what the applicant is prepared to do rather than what he or she has already accomplished.

This style is useful for individuals who:

- Are changing careers or changing the emphasis of their career and need to highlight qualifications gained through work that may not be obviously related to the job vacancy.

- Have just completed their education and training.

- Are reentering the job market.

- Have held several positions with very similar job descriptions and, therefore, find it difficult to differentiate between jobs or show progress on the job.

**Combination of functional and chronological.** Some individuals need to demonstrate their work history *and* highlight their specific qualifications. For example, a physician who has been in direct patient care in several settings is applying for a job that requires management skills. The resume should include both a description of the jobs performed in each setting (chronological style) and a listing of management skills acquired (functional style). A combination style resume is an effective method of providing guidance to interviewers who may have difficulty understanding how the practice of medicine equips one with skills that are useful in other settings.

Chapter Two provides assistance in writing each major element of your resume.

# Writing your resume

## Heading

The heading is the simplest section of your resume. It highlights your name and provides all the information a potential employer needs to contact you for an interview.

Make your name stand out. Capitalize all the letters and use boldface type. Skip a line and insert your address, phone, and fax numbers. Cite your e-mail address, particularly if you are planning to emphasize your computer skills. A heading with a single address would look like this.

---

**Kenneth W. Rodgers, MD**

1401 Riverside Drive
Elmwood, IN 50931
Phone: 555-341-8734
Fax: 555-341-9942
e-mail: krodgers@xyz.com

---

If you wish to be contacted at your office or if you have both a temporary and a permanent address, consider putting both listings in the heading. However, if you wish *not* to be contacted at work, be sure to say so. Even if you don't supply the address or phone number of your current office, an eager recruiter can find them.

```
┌─────────────────────────────────────────────────────────────┐
│                  Kenneth W. Rodgers, MD                      │
│                                                              │
│   Home:                          Office:                     │
│   1401 Riverside Drive           Metropolitan Medical Group  │
│   Elmwood, IN 50931              Suite 402                    │
│   Phone: 555-341-8734            5318 Terrace Road            │
│   Fax: 555-341-9942              Terre Haute, IN 59032        │
│   e-mail: krodgers@xyz.com       Phone: 555-247-5039          │
│                                  Fax: 555-247-5111            │
│                                                              │
└─────────────────────────────────────────────────────────────┘
```

If you are using both a temporary and a permanent address:

```
┌─────────────────────────────────────────────────────────────┐
│                  Kenneth W. Rodgers, MD                      │
│                                                              │
│   Until June 30, 1998:           After July 1, 1998:         │
│   1401 Riverside Drive           Metropolitan Medical Group  │
│   Elmwood, IN 50931              Suite 402                    │
│   Phone: 555-341-8734            5318 Terrace Road            │
│   Fax: 555-341-9942              Terre Haute, IN 59032        │
│   e-mail: krodgers@xyz.com       Phone: 555-247-5039          │
│                                  Fax: 555-247-5111            │
│                                                              │
└─────────────────────────────────────────────────────────────┘
```

While your name is prominently displayed on the first page of your resume, be sure to put it on every page. All subsequent pages should have either a footer or a header that repeats your name and shows the page number of the resume.

For a good appearance, leave about one inch of white space above your name; skip at least three lines below the heading before beginning the next section. You may prefer a horizontal line to set off the heading or a heading that is left-aligned as shown below.

```
┌─────────────────────────────────────────────────────────────┐
│                  Kenneth W. Rodgers, MD                      │
│                                                              │
│   1401 Riverside Drive           Phone: 555-341-8734         │
│   Elmwood, IN 50931              Fax: 555-341-9942           │
│                                  e-mail: krodgers@xyz.com    │
│                                                              │
└─────────────────────────────────────────────────────────────┘
```

Whether centered or left-aligned, the heading information should be presented clearly and concisely with emphasis on your name. Keep it simple—no gimmicks.

## Do

- Be sure that the phone you listed will be answered during regular business hours or that it is connected to an answering machine. If necessary, note the times during the day when it will be answered. If you are sending out a large number of resumes, it pays to have an answering machine installed.

- Spell out all the information in the address. Don't use St, Ave, Ct, etc. Spell out everything simply because it looks better. You may use the two-letter postal abbreviation for states.

- Make the header—the first item a recruiter sees—look professional.

- Double-check every phone and fax number you list.

- If you include an e-mail address, be sure to check frequently for messages.

## Don't

- Label the first page "Resume" or "Curriculum Vitae"—just put your name at the top.

- Add any fancy graphics or typefaces. A resume is serious business.

# Job objective

About 50% of the authors of books on how to write resumes declare that every resume should include a job objective. The other 50% tell you to omit it because it may narrow recruiters' perceptions of your interests.

A job objective is a simple statement of what you want to do and why you are qualified to do it. A stated objective might be particularly elucidating if your resume doesn't seem to fit the job for which you are applying. But it can be restrictive if the objective is so narrow that only one perfect job will fit.

> ## Tip
>
> You probably need to write an objective if:
>
> - You are seeking your first job after completing your education. The objective allows you to set the parameters of the placement you seek (eg, size, type, and location of a medical group or other practice opportunity).
>
> - You are changing directions in your career. For example, if you have been involved in patient care for the past 10 years and have decided that you want to go into full-time teaching of allied health personnel, that objective should be clearly stated. Otherwise, your background is going to seem irrelevant to the job or you may be considered overqualified.
>
> - You want a more challenging position. Ready to move into management? Looking for entrepreneurial opportunities? If so, state your objective accordingly.
>
> - You have very specific job requirements and will accept nothing else. For example, if, for family health reasons, you must be located in a particular section of the country, include the geographical location in your objective.

If you decide that your presentation will benefit from inclusion of a job objective, you have two options: (1) carefully craft a statement that can be included in your resume or (2) include the same statement in the cover letter used to transmit your resume to a prospective employer. If you choose to write an objective, make sure it is clearly stated, specific, and brief. Here are some examples.

**Sample Job Objectives**

- An academic position in a major allied health school where I can use my teaching experience and interest in the use of physician extenders

- A senior management position in a managed care organization where I can use my knowledge of and experience in working with large medical groups

- Research activities that take advantage of my experience in working with geriatric patients

- Participation in a small orthopedic practice in the Southwest

- To join an academic medical practice where I can use my patient care skills, my interest in teaching pediatrics, and my experience in conducting research projects.

- To work in a multispecialty group providing care to an underserved population or geographic area

- To join a primary care practice in a small or rural community

- To obtain a two-year appointment in emergency medicine in the Boston area before entering a medical/business administration program

The job objective is usually listed immediately after the heading, centered or left justified, and separated from other text by one or two lines of white space. This is one section of your resume where the use of I, my, and me is appropriate.

If you are uncertain of your objective or find it hard to put into words, leave it out of your resume. You may find it easier to state your objective in a cover letter when you are responding to a specific advertisement or job.

# Education

The education section of your resume begins with undergraduate school (skip high school—we all know you made it past that step) and covers at least your formal education. It may also include internships, residencies, and fellowships. Informal and continuing education courses can be listed under education if they are directly relevant to your job objective or can be added at the end of your resume.

Each entry should contain at least the name of the school from which you received a degree, the location (city and state), the date of your degree (unless it was conferred more than twenty years ago), and the dates of attendance if there were gaps in your education or if you attended more than one college or university before receiving a degree. Recruiters always look for gaps in education or work history. Explain the gaps so that the recruiter focuses on what you accomplished and not on the lapses. You may choose to cite honors after each degree, or you may want to add a section for honors at the end of your resume.

## Tip

If you have little or no work experience, you may want to list internships, residencies, and fellowships in your work history rather than in the education section. This gives you an opportunity to describe in some detail the content of your training programs.

As demonstrated in the following examples, several formats can be used to show your educational background. All are appropriate. Choose the one that looks best with the rest of your resume. For example, if your heading is centered, center the education section; if left-justified, be consistent in continuing that justification. Note that in these examples, the dates of attendance follow the name of the institution. If the dates are listed first in a left-hand column, they appear to be more important than the remainder of the information.

---

### EDUCATION

| | |
|---|---|
| College: | Columbia University, New York, NY<br>Bachelor of Science in Biology, with honors, 1973 |
| Medical School: | State University of New York, Brooklyn, NY<br>Medical Doctor, 1977 |
| Internship: | State University of New York, Brooklyn, NY<br>Surgical Intern, 1977 - 1978 |
| Residency: | George Washington University, Washington, DC<br>General Surgery, 1978 - 1980 |
| Fellowship: | Temple University Hospital, Philadelphia, PA<br>Surgery, 1980 - 1981 |

---

## EDUCATION

Columbia University, New York, NY
Bachelor of Science in Physics, 1973, cum laude

State University of New York Medical School, New York, NY
MD, 1977

State University of New York, Brooklyn, NY
Surgery Intern, 1977 - 1978

George Washington University, Washington, DC
General Surgery Resident, 1978 - 1980

Temple University Hospital, Philadelphia, PA
Surgery Fellowship, 1980 - 1981

Some resumes separate undergraduate and medical education from postgraduate training, as shown below.

## EDUCATION

| Degree | Institution | Year |
|--------|-------------|------|
| BS | University of Cincinnati, Cincinnati, OH | 1967 |
| MD | University of Cincinnati, Cincinnati, OH College of Medicine | 1971 |

## POSTGRADUATE TRAINING

| Position | Institution | Year |
|----------|-------------|------|
| Resident | Indiana University, Bloomington, IN Internal Medicine | 1971 - 1974 |
| Fellow | University of Osceola, Osceola, IN Nephrology | 1974 - 1976 |

If you prefer your resume left-justified, here's a simple, alternative format.

## EDUCATION

Duke University, Raleigh, NC (1989 - 1993)
BS in Biology, 1993
Dean's List all semesters

Duke University, Raleigh, NC (1993 - 1997)
MD, 1997

## Tip

If you have just completed your education and have not held a job in medicine or a related field that you wish to highlight, add a phrase under each of your degrees to amplify the experience. Include such items as these:

- Special honors or awards (summa or magna cum laude)
- Grade point average (if above a 3.0) or Dean's List
- Participation in exchange programs (particularly if this led to fluency in a second language)
- Scholarships
- Teaching assistantships or other special positions
- Incidentals such as leadership positions, early graduation, or that you worked your way through school
- Ranking in your graduation class, eg, third in a class of 240

In general, use these items sparingly and only if your education is recent. Exception: If you are applying for an academic position, show all your academic honors no matter how long ago they occurred. Be sure that whatever you mention enhances your resume and is not added for length alone.

## Do

- List all formal education, degrees granted, and institutions.
- Emphasize the institutions and the degrees—not the dates of attendance.

## Don't

- Overuse honors, awards, and other embellishments.
- Be inconsistent in the format used.

# Highlights, skills, and accomplishments

If you are preparing a functional style resume, the highlights, skills, and accomplishments section is crucial. If you are seeking a job for the first time since completing your education, if you are changing direction in your career, or if you are reentering the job market after a period of absence, call attention to your competencies or highlight a few of your skills that are pertinent to the type of job you are seeking. Also, in this section, mention those qualifications that you gained outside your work history, such as management experience obtained in doing community or volunteer work.

If you are preparing a combination style resume because your work history is either static (only one employer and a single job description for a long period of time) or repetitious (several jobs with basically the same content), this section emphasizes the skills that you accumulated while holding those jobs. For example, if you have been in private practice either solo or in a small group, your job descriptions may be short—even assumed by most readers. But you probably acquired business and management skills that are not apparent from the job description. Highlight these skills in this section of your resume. Your work history section will not include extensive job descriptions but will note only employers, job titles, and dates of employment.

A chronological style resume does not require that this section be included. You may choose to include it, however, to emphasize competencies that you have gained that may not appear in your work history. For example, you may be an effective negotiator—experience gained through practice mergers, acquisitions, or PHO formation—but not necessarily reflected in the description of your job.

As you write this section, keep these cautions in mind:

- Every statement should relate to your goals and objectives in getting a job. While you may play the violin exceptionally well, that skill is probably not going to help you get a job managing a multispecialty clinic.

- Include no more than four or five highlights, each of which should be one or two sentences or phrases long.

- Be sure that the work history, education, or personal interest sections of your resume identify how you obtained the skills you list in this section.

- Keep in mind that the primary purpose of this section is to draw the interviewer/recruiter's eye to the most important points about your candidacy.

Here are some examples with an alternative title, Career Highlights. Other titles that you might use are Skills and Accomplishments, Areas of Expertise, Selected Accomplishments, or Recent Accomplishments.

---

### Sample Career Highlights

- Successfully developed and implemented management information systems to support all business aspects of a multispecialty medical group practice; system includes automated clinical records.

- Proven ability to develop new business relationships; increased managed care contracts from one to five in two years and integrated the patients and business processes without a disruption in operations.

- Considerable background teaching allied health personnel how to instruct patients in self-care techniques and uses of medical products.

- Awarded Randall Fellowship for outstanding performance during residency.

- Graduated third in medical school at Duke University in a class of 150 students.

- Performed extensive research on medical products and pharmaceuticals used in the care of diabetics.

---

The highlights, skills, and accomplishments section usually appears immediately after the heading or job objective. Like your name in the heading, this section should stand out so it catches the attention of the lazy-eyed reader. The highlights section should be set off by two lines of white space above and below the text.

# Work history

Work history is a necessary element of every physician's resume. The only resume writers who are exempt from preparing a work history are those rare individuals who never held a job—and even they might have held a few part-time or volunteer jobs worth noting.

Begin by collecting the information you need about each of your previous and current positions: employer's company name, location (city and state), dates of employment, job title, and job description. While you are pulling the information together, make a separate list of the mailing address or phone number for each of your employers. Although you won't use employers' addresses in the resume, the information may come in handy when you're compiling your list of references.

Before deciding how to format and list the jobs, write a description of the work you performed at each company (or in self-employment). Use present tense to describe your current job and past tense for the others. Never use I or me—everyone knows by now that this is your resume. Each description should be clear, concise, and action oriented.

In the left-hand column of the following table are examples of how physicians might have described their jobs before reading this book. The descriptions are bland and self-effacing, and they communicate little about the resume writer. In the right-hand column, those descriptions have been rewritten to be more action oriented, to show the skills and accomplishments of the writer, and to create a more complete picture of physicians' work. As you can see, the writers made these descriptions clear, concise, and action oriented.

| Before: Typical Rendition | After: Improved Version |
|---|---|
| In private practice of medicine; first as a solo practitioner and later in a group of 10 physicians. | Built a medical practice (family practice) from 1 physician to 10 physicians (and 21 ancillary staff) in 14 years. Created management systems, trained staff, negotiated employment arrangements and service contracts with insurance companies, HMOs, and PHOs. Developed two satellite offices. Manage largest of the three offices and care for patients three days per week. |
| House Physician engaged in the practice of cardiology. | As House Physician in a 420-bed urban hospital, evaluated patients with potential cardiac problems, initiated emergency care, and coordinated follow-up with private physicians. Performed more than 700 angiograms and nearly 300 PTCAs. Published 9 research papers and conducted 12 educational programs during this two-year assignment. |
| Clinical Pharmacologist with teaching assignments in the Departments of Medicine and Pharmacology. | Hold dual professorships in medicine and pharmacology. Developed oncology consulting service for community hospitals. Supervise and teach house staff and medical students on clinical clerkships. Serve as physician-in-charge of 5 to 10 oncology inpatients and outpatients, most of whom are in advanced stages of their disease. |

| | |
|---|---|
| Pediatrician in a primary care practice. | Served a panel of primary care pediatric patients (up to age 16); counseled other family practice physicians in the group on pediatric problems; created a pediatric infectious disease program to serve all pediatric patients in the practice; obtained grants for several research programs in infectious disease. |
| Fellow in Nephrology and Hypertension. | Participate in a clinically based program covering all phases of nephrology, including hemodialysis, transplantation, CAPD, and consultation. Upon completion of the fellowship, will have performed approximately 15 biopsies, 70 catheter accesses, and 150 peritoneal catheter placements. |

Many recruiters appreciate job descriptions that use a format of bulleted statements. The first example above could easily be converted to a bulleted format.

Metropolitan Medical Group, Hamilton, OH (1983 to present)
Founding Partner

- Built a medical practice (family medicine) from 1 physician to 10 in 14 years.

- Created management systems, trained staff, negotiated employment arrangements and service contracts with insurance companies, HMOs, and PHOs.

- Developed two satellite offices.

- Manage the largest of the three offices and care for patients three days per week.

A word about format. Whatever is on the left side of the paper will get the most attention since we read English from left to right. The jobs that you performed are far more important in capturing the attention of the recruiter than the dates. So it makes sense to list the employer or organization and your title on the left, followed by the dates. Either your job title or your employer can be listed first, depending on whether you think the recruiter will be more impressed with your title or the organization's name. Be consistent throughout your resume in using this order.

Using the information about the founding partner of Metropolitan Medical Group, shown above, here is how the complete work history might look.

---

## WORK HISTORY

Metropolitan Medical Group, Hamilton, OH (1983 to present)
Founding Partner

- Built a medical practice (family practice) from 1 physician to 10 physicians (and 21 ancillary staff) in 14 years.

- Created management systems, trained staff, negotiated employment arrangements and service contracts with insurance companies, HMOs, and PHOs.

- Developed two satellite offices.

- Manage the largest of the three offices and care for patients three days per week.

Oakwood Medical Center, Columbus, OH (1979 to 1983)
Partner

- Provided care to local families with a special interest in care for the elderly; three-person practice.

- Initiated a home-based hospice and served as its medical director for one year (1983).

United States Navy (1973 to 1979)
Lieutenant Commander

- Was Assistant Clinical Professor, Naval Regional Medical Center.

---

Here are some points to remember when you are writing your work history.

- The name and location of the employer should be listed without abbreviations—except for the postal designations for states.

- List your title or, if the title does not describe the content of your work, leave it out and simply describe your duties.

- The dates can be written as month and year or years only. If you have a few gaps in your work history, use only the years throughout your resume.

- Start with your current or most recent job and work backward. If you have had a full career, list all the jobs held in the past fifteen to twenty years. Skip any jobs that you held over twenty years ago or summarize them.

- If you have held part-time jobs concurrently, note that with the overlapping dates of each. For example:

  Union Hospital (part-time, 1992 - 1994)
  House Officer

  City Ambulatory Clinic (part-time, 1992 - 1994)
  Emergency Room Clerk

**Do**

- Use present tense for your current job; use past tense in describing previous jobs.

- Quantify your experience wherever possible—number of procedures, amount of budget, increases in services.

- Use active verbs when describing your work history. If you need prompting, review the list of active verbs shown in Appendix A.

- Be consistent in your format.

- Include military service in your work history.

- Use bullets wherever appropriate. Bulleted lists stand out better than full sentences.

- Begin your work history with your current or last job and work backward; cover fifteen to twenty years of experience *if* it is relevant.

**Don't**

- Use I, me, or my when writing your job descriptions. Begin each phrase with an active verb.

- Indicate why you left your previous jobs.

- Provide past employers' names and addresses or cite your salary history.

## Personal interests

Citing some of your personal interests and activities helps show a prospective interviewer that you are a well-rounded applicant. Interests might include sports, community involvement, hobbies, leadership positions held, volunteer work, and artistic or creative endeavors, to name a few. Here are some guidelines for deciding what to include.

- Match the interests that you list in your resume with the type of job you are seeking. If you are seeking a job in an aggressive company or industry, mention your competitive interests. If you are headed for academia, highlight your intellectual interests. If you do not actively participate in anything but work, skip this element.

- Keep your statements short unless you can cite some outstanding accomplishments. Let's say you are an avid runner and have entered six marathons in the past ten years with a personal best time of three hours and eighteen minutes. Brag about your accomplishment. Simply listing running as an interest adds little to your resume.

- Don't include interests that reveal religious or political preferences unless you can relate some of those activities to your employment search. Let's say that you have spearheaded a highly successful fund-raising drive for your church, raising $500,000 in 18 months. Shout it out, but don't bother to mention the church's denomination.

- Note important, recent leadership positions that are linked to your interests. Chairman of a community group or neighborhood association, council member for a youth group, or coordinator of a sports event are all good choices of experiences that show you are an active leader. Leadership positions held in professional organizations are usually noted in the section on professional societies and committees.

- If you actively participate in sports, note the sport and how you are involved. Perhaps you serve as a coach—if you coached a winning team, be sure to say so. Or perhaps you are an avid golfer. If you can add that you organize local golfing tournaments or something unusual about your involvement in the sport, all the better.

- Your creative interests can shine here, too. Are you an expert chef who specializes in Cajun cooking? Have you won a prize in a photography contest? Did the antique automobile that you restored win first prize at the concourse in the last auto show? Do you play in the local symphony or a jazz band or sing torch songs?

- List at least one active interest. Saying that you like camping, travel, and cycling is rather dull. Saying that you like to camp and specialize in camping at elevations of twelve thousand feet or more, indicating that you have made seven trips to Italy in ten years and now are fluent in Italian, or stating that your interest in cycling has led you to establish a free bicycle clinic for kids in your neighborhood all sound like active interests and help to describe a full life.

Short phrases are the best format for listing interests. The suggestions listed above might look like this:

---

**Sample Personal Interests**

- Avid runner. Entered six marathons in past ten years; personal best time of three hours and eighteen minutes.

- Co-authored a 100-year history of our neighborhood.

- Chaired a church fund-raising committee; raised $500,000 in 18 months.

- Create sculptures in metal and wood.

- Vice president of the Kent Neighborhood Association; formerly served as treasurer.

- Reading the classics; currently enrolled in a Great Books discussion group.

- Coach women's softball team; team has been in semifinals of the county league every year for the past four years.

- Enjoy cooking Cajun food; gave Cajun cooking classes on local television for two years.

- Write children's stories.

- Traveled to Italy seven times in the past ten years in order to gain fluency in Italian.

---

Your personal interests bring your resume alive and make recruiters want to know more about you.

> **Do**
>
> - List active pursuits and note accomplishments.
> - Select the types of interests that relate to your job goals wherever possible.
>
> **Don't**
>
> - Reveal religious or political preferences.
> - Be vague. Saying that you like sports does not enhance your resume.

## Licenses, certifications, and appointments

List each of the states in which you are licensed to practice medicine; show the license number and date of expiration. Even if you only wish to work in one state, list all your licenses. Note all board certifications, dates attained, and expiration dates (if any). Appointments to academic training programs should be noted with dates. A simple list is the proper format. If you are a young physician in the process of becoming certified, but have not yet received your certification, state where in the certification process you currently are (eg, written boards, oral boards, awaiting results, board eligible).

**Licenses**
California, #56910 (expires 12/99)
Kansas, #9023 (expires 6/98)

**Licenses**
California, #56910, 1978 to present
Kansas, #9023, 1981 to present

**Certifications**
American Board of Internal Medicine, 1991
Diplomate American Board of Plastic Surgery, 1978
Advanced Cardiac Life Support Provider, 1989 - present

**Appointments**

Assistant Clinical Professor, Naval Regional Medical Center
(1985 - 1988)
Professor of Medicine, University of Iowa Medical School
(1995 - present)

# References

Most prospective employers do not expect you to submit a list of references with your resume. They do, however, expect that you will, on request, provide a list of people who will give you a reference. Usually a recruiter will ask for your list of references during your interview or as a follow-up to the interview.

Choose references that you know will speak well of you and who know you and/or your work well. Type a list that includes accurate, current addresses and phone numbers and be prepared to present the list at the close of your first interview. (See Appendix B for a sample reference list.)

## Tip

A good list of references might contain:

- Three personal references who can verify that you are an upstanding, stable citizen. These might include attorneys, accountants, business owners, and others who may know you not only from business relationships with your practice but through social contact with you as well.

- Three medical colleagues who can verify your professional abilities. The medical director or administrator of a hospital, physicians who are not members of your practice group, PHO officers, and professors (particularly if you have just finished your education) might be appropriate references.

Contact your references in advance to obtain their permission to give their names as references and ensure that they understand the circumstances surrounding your job search. You may wish to keep your job search quiet until you have found the right job—so caution your references that you do not want your present employer or partners to know of your search. Help them prepare your references by explaining the type of job you are seeking and how you think your background fits the job.

Do not ask for letters of reference in advance (unless one of your references is so powerful that his or her backing would get you the job immediately). Even if you have such letters available, recruiters will probably ask you to prepare a list of individuals they can contact personally.

On your resume, simply put "References provided upon request." Do not include the list of names with your resume. Have it available at the interview or agree to send it immediately after the interview.

## Other sections

What about all the other things you do or have done that are not "officially" part of your job? Should you list your presentations, memberships in professional societies, or publications? The answer is both yes and no. Yes, you should list some of the extracurricular professional activities that are related to your job objective. No, you probably should not list every committee on which you have served for the past fifteen years.

In preparing the first draft of your resume, list the *most recent or most important extracurricular activities* that fall under these categories:

- Honors and awards
- Professional societies/offices held
- Committees
- Publications
- Editorships
- Research
- Presentations
- Special skills
- Special training (after formal education)

Here are some suggestions of what to consider that may help refresh your memory.

## Honors and Awards

- Graduated summa cum laude from undergraduate and medical school

- Phi Beta Kappa

- BS in Biology with honors

- First rank in MBBS examination

- Who's Who in the East, 1994

- First prize: Keasey Memorial Resident Essay Contest, 1993

- Woman of the Year, Poolesville Rotary Club, 1995

Remember, you can also list honors and awards in the section on education.

## Professional Societies/Offices Held

American Medical Association

Local medical societies

American College of Physicians (Member)

National Kidney Foundation, Publications Committee Chair

American Academy of Pediatrics, Regional Delegate

International Microsurgery Society

Society of Nuclear Medicine (Fellow)

American College of Physician Executives (Member)

## Committees

Oncology Strategy Working Group, Memorial Hospital, 1991 - 1993

Credentialing Committee, Family Health Plan, 1994 - present

Chairman, Decubitus Ulcer Task Force, Andersonville Hospital, 1995

Managed Care Task Force, American College of Radiology,
    1994 - 1996

Participation on committees shows a willingness to help solve organizational and institutional problems and an ability to work with others and can highlight leadership skills. Clearly, serving on committees of national scientific organizations carries more prestige than serving hospital, HMO, or PHO committees, but you may wish to list all of your current commitments and those of importance in the recent past.

## Publications/Editorships

Publications can support your job search if used appropriately. Before revising or updating your list of publications, see if one of the situations listed in the left-hand column of the following table describes you. Then, read the information in the right-hand column for advice on the best way to list your publications on your resume.

| Situation | How to Handle |
|---|---|
| You have a few publications that are pertinent to your job search. | List your publications in a separate section on your resume. |
| You have many publications but most are more than ten years old. | List your publications in a separate document and note on your resume that a list of publications is available on request. |
| You are applying for an academic position. | List all your publications, regardless of date, in a separate document and append it to your resume. |
| You are a frequent author but do not feel there is a need to list all your publications (eg, some are not relevant to your job search). | Summarize your publishing contributions and note them in your resume (eg, authored 40 scientific articles, edited a book on spinal surgery, contributed 12 book chapters on orthopedic surgery, and numerous articles for lay journals, magazines, and public information brochures). |
| You have publications that are not pertinent to the job you are seeking. | List your publications in a separate document and note on your resume that a list of publications is available on request. |

Keep in mind that every journal, society, and academic institution establishes its own style guide for listing publications. It makes little difference which you use as long as you use it consistently. If you have a publications list already prepared, check it for currency and consistency and continue to use it.

For those who have not prepared a list of publications previously, a fairly simple format for doing so is shown in Appendix C.

## Editorships

Assistant Editor, *Journal of Endourology*
Reviewer, *Archives of Internal Medicine*
Member of the Editorial Board, *The Medical Letter*

## Research

If you are applying for a research position, list the grants and projects on which you have worked. If you have participated in a number of projects, you may need to create a separate document similar to your list of publications. The grants list should include the title of the research project, the donor of the grant, your title while working on the grant (eg, co-investigator), and the dates. Your list of research projects should reflect similar information, plus the name of the primary investigator if that was someone other than you, and whether or not the research resulted in a publication (eg, published in the March 1989 issue of *JAMA*).

The following samples show how two types of entries for grants and research projects might be mentioned in your resume (if there are only a few) or aggregated in a research list (if there are many).

"Geriatric Surgical Patients: An Audit of 500 Patients," with Jane S. Williams, MD, William Beaumont Hospital, Royal Oak, MI (February 1983 to November 1993).

Research grant from the Conley Foundation to study the effectiveness of perinatal care in community hospitals and academic teaching facilities. Research conducted with James H. Henley, MD, at the University of Colorado, 1993 - 1995.

University of Oregon Medical School, Department of Psychiatry, Richard B. Ballou, MD. "Systems of Care for Children and Adolescents with Emotional Disorders," 1995 to present.

With Kaye M. Williams, MD, MPH: Research project in the socioeconomic differences in lung cancer incidence. Washington County Department of Health, Washington, WV, 1991 to 1993.

### Sample Grant Support

Department of Medicine, Commonwealth of Pennsylvania
Robert Wood Johnson Foundation
Upjohn Pharmaceutical Laboratory
Berlex, Inc
Medical Research Foundation of California

### Tip

- Use a listing of research projects when the content of the research is important to your job search.

- Use a list of supporting grantors when your ability to attract research funds is important.

Academic institutions often specify the manner in which research projects are reported. If you have used such a style in the past, continue to use it on your resume or list of research projects. Otherwise, choose one of the sample styles shown and follow it consistently in listing your research efforts. Keep in mind that, if research is not an important part of your background or if you are not interested in pursuing research, summarize your research experience in a sentence or two. These sentences can stand alone under the heading of research or can become part of your job descriptions.

If you have conducted several research projects but are not emphasizing those interests, a statement that you participated in several research projects in a stated subject is sufficient. Offer to provide a list of those projects, if requested. Then be sure to assemble the information so it is ready at the time of your interview.

## Presentations

Presentations are included on your resume either in summary form or as separate citations. If teaching is an important part of your job quest, develop a list of recent (past 10 years maximum) seminars, workshops, and other presentations. Give the title, sponsoring organization, location, and date. Summarizing is certainly acceptable, such as: conducted 35 seminars, workshops, and formal presentations on new urological surgery techniques over the past 10 years; these presentations were for physician audiences at local, national, and international meetings.

## Special Skills

If you have a special skill that enhances your candidacy and is not obvious from your work history and education, list it here. Below are examples showing skills in computers and languages.

Information management: developed software to support various medical practice business functions; skilled in using numerous commercially available statistical research software packages.

On-line research for both clinical and nonclinical subjects.

Fluent in German; speak, read, write, translate, and interpret.

Expert in lip reading; moderately fluent in sign language.

## Special Training

While it is not recommended that you list all the continuing medical education courses you have taken over the years, you may have special training that is applicable to your job search.

Critical Care Management—six-day course, University of North Carolina, 1993.

The Management of Group Practices—six-week program at University of Colorado School of Business, 1983.

Dynamic Video Display of Ischemic Heart Disease with MRI—Roetgen Ray Society, Omaha, NE, April 1994.

# Putting the pieces together

If you have followed the suggestions in this text, you have drafted the pieces for your resume. Now you need to put them together in a professional looking document and critique the result.

- If you don't have access to a word processor and a letter quality printer, find a commercial organization that can help you. Most large copying shops offer printing services. If you don't have an easy way to prepare, edit, and rearrange the elements in your resume, this will be an onerous task. Get help.

- Assemble the pieces in what appears to you to be a logical order. Clearly, the heading goes first, probably followed by the job objective, if you are using one. Accomplishments might be next, followed by education and work history. After that, the order of the extras is immaterial. Imagine that you are reading the resume for the first time. Does the order flow logically from basic information to the more important aspects of your career? Are your accomplishments highlighted?

- Ask yourself if the resume seems too long. Without attachments, resumes for a recent graduate should be one to two pages in length. For physicians with a full career (without attachments such as publications, research grants, etc), three to four pages long is the rule of thumb. If yours is longer and you are satisfied with the way it looks and reads, don't worry about length.

- Evaluate every section. Polish the wording. Check for spelling, grammar, and punctuation errors. Look for inconsistencies in the manner in which the information is presented (eg, all the listings in the work history list job titles and dates in the same way).

- Look at all the extras, such as presentations or honors. If they need only a few lines, perhaps they can be merged with other sections of your resume. For example, honors and awards might become part of the education segment; teaching responsibilities might be mentioned under work history. Perhaps the publications, editorships, and committees can be shortened, deleted, or made into a separate document, available on request.

- Edit, edit, edit. First make sure that each paragraph presents an accurate picture of you and your talents—and does so as succinctly as possible. Take another look at the list of action verbs in Appendix A and use them.

- Compare your resume with the examples in the next section. Does the comparison suggest any changes in format or wording?

- Have someone else—or more than one person—critique the final product. Ask them to check for consistency in format, comment on the wording, and proofread for errors. If they know you well, ask them to comment on whether or not your resume represents you well. Your spouse, a colleague, a friend, or your teenage children might conduct the review.

Appendix D contains an evaluation tool to help you check your efforts against all the suggestions that were made in this section on preparing your resume. Use it to see if your have forgotten anything—and have others use it to evaluate your work. When you are satisfied with the result, print a copy of your resume to refer to as you move on to the next step—developing cover letters to transmit your beautiful resume to potential employers.

# Resume writing exercise

## Five resumes—before and after: An exercise

Following are resumes for five physicians who are seeking employment. To help you learn to spot poorly prepared or unattractively presented resumes, each sample is presented first with some flaws in content and format—the *Before* version.

Read the first *Before* resume and note the errors and problems. Then check yourself by reading the answers and comments that follow each example to see if you caught all the boners.

Look at the first *After* resume. The improvements in content and format should be obvious. Each of the *After* resumes notes the style and the font used to create the resume, as well as the suggested type size. The fonts used are common ones that should be available on your personal or office word processor or from any of the printing and copying shops that can help you format and print your resume.

Repeat the exercise with each of the five resumes. Seeing these common mistakes will help you to develop your own—perfect—resume.

# John M. Wengley, MD

**2861 Arizona Avenue**
**Washington, DC 55324**
Phone: 555-341-8734
Fax: 555-341-8734

**Job Objective:**

To leave the private practice of medicine and teach in a medical center

**Education:**

| | |
|---|---|
| Medical Degree | Chicago Medical School<br>North Chicago, IL, 1975 - June 1979 |
| College | Columbia University<br>New York, NY 1971 - 1975 |
| Internship | Cook County Hospital<br>Chicago, IL 1979 - 1980 |
| Residency | State University of New York<br>Brooklyn, NY 1980 - 1984 |

**Job Hisotry:**

| | |
|---|---|
| 1984 - present | Orthopedic Surgeon in Chicago, IL<br>Worked in a five-man orthopedics practice. Licensed in Illinois and Iowa. Board certified in Orthopedics. |

**Professional Organizations**

American Medical Association (Member)
Illinois State Medical Society
Chicago Medical Society

**Personal Interests**

Fishing, hiking.

**Special Training:**

Isolated Fractures of the Tibial Eminence, University of Illinois, 1993
Review Course in Prosthetics, University of Iowa, 1994

**Personal:**

Date of birth: January 15, 1952
Married to June Davis Wengley
Three children:   Juliet, age 12
                  James, age 9
                  Jennifer, age 8

## Resume 1—Comments

Dr. Wengley must be a very shy individual. This resume tells us little about him.

- The objective is not well stated. It is always in poor taste to cite a negative as a goal (to leave the private practice of medicine).

- Some of the subheads are followed by a colon; others are not. Be consistent

- Typographical error (Job HIsotry). Proofread carefully.

- Fax and phone number are the same. While some machines do use the same number, it is more likely that one number is in error. Check all numbers as part of your proofreading.

- The punctuation in the education section is inconsistent.

- The order of the listings in education is inconsistent. Choose either reverse chronological or chronological order and stick with it.

- The job listing is poorly done:
    It doesn't contain action words or phrases.
    It gives little information about the nature of the practice.
    It begins with the dates of service, drawing attention to the time period rather than the content of the job.
    A ten-year job history should be more prominently displayed or highlighted.
    The description uses the past tense but the job is current.

- The personal interests as stated are not worth listing.

- The length of the training programs is not cited.

- Personal data should not be part of a resume.

# John M. Wengley, MD

**2861 Arizona Avenue**
**Washington, DC 55324**
Phone: 555-341-8734
Fax: 555-341-8755

## Job Objective:

An academic position in a major allied health school where I can use my teaching experience and interest in the use of physician extenders.

## Education:

| | |
|---|---|
| College | Columbia University<br>New York, NY (1971 - 1975)<br>B.S. in Chemistry; with honors |
| Medical Degree | Chicago Medical School<br>North Chicago, IL (1975 - 1979) |
| Internship | Cook County Hospital<br>Chicago, IL (1979 - 1980) |
| Residency | State University of New York<br>Brooklyn, NY (1980 - 1984) |

## Job History:

Orthopedic Surgeon
Metropolitan Orthopedics
Chicago, IL

(1984 - present)

Provide general orthopedic care in a busy practice of five orthopedists and a support staff of 25. Work extensively with physician assistants, orthotic technicians, prosthetists, physical therapists, and registered nurses. Developed and taught courses in nursing skills for registered nurses working in orthopedic practices (University of Illinois School of Nursing). Established and supervised on-the-job training of all ancillary staff in the practice. In conjunction with the orthotic technicians and prosthetists, created an education program for families with members who are dependent on wheelchairs or orthotic devices. Given the Physician of the Year Award by Memorial Hospital in 1994 for work with device-dependent patients.

**Professional Organizations:**

American Medical Association (Member)
Illinois State Medical Society (Former Economics Committee Chair)
Chicago Medical Society (President-elect)

**Personal Interests:**

Avid outdoor enthusiast. Particularly interested in fishing and hiking; volunteer
as a weekend counselor with an organization that provides outdoor experiences to
inner-city children.

**Special Training:**

Isolated Fractures of the Tibial Eminence, four-day course at University of Illinois, 1993
Review Course in Prosthetics, two-week update at University of Iowa, 1994

**Licenses / Certifications:**

Illinois license number: 42847
Iowa license number: WE 44982
American Board of Orthopaedic Surgery: Diplomate, 1985

**Presentations:**

During the past six years, presented more than 30 short courses on orthopedic techniques,
orthotics, protheses, and use of orthopedic devices. The audiences ranged from
physicians to technicians and nurses to wheelchair-bound patients and their families.

References and a list of recent presentations are available on request.

Times New Roman, 10 pt.
Chronological style

## CURRICULUM VITAE: MARVIN WILLIAMS, MD

| | |
|---|---|
| DATE OF BIRTH: | 3 October, 1956 |
| PLACE OF BIRTH: | Johnston, OH |
| CITIZENSHIP: | U.S.A. |
| SOCIAL SECURITY NO.: | 378-04-6785 |
| MARITAL STATUS: | Married to Carolyn Williams |
| CHILDREN: | Bobby Williams (age 3) |
| | Carin Williams (age 18 months) |
| HOME ADDRESS: | 2451 Locust Street |
| | Galen, IL 33789 |
| JOB OBJECTIVE: | To join an existing practice as a pediatrician. |
| ACCOMPLISHMENTS: | Completed a residency in pediatrics with high recommendations from the faculty |

EDUCATION:

| | |
|---|---|
| 1981 - 1986 | Tennessee University |
| | Jackson, TN |
| | B.S., Biology, graduated cum laude |
| 1986 - 1990 | Tennessee University |
| | Jackson, TN |
| | Doctor of Medicine |
| 1990 - 1991 | Intern in Pediatrics |
| | East Carolina University |
| | Greenville, NC |
| 1991 - 1993 | East Carolina University |
| | Greenville, NC |
| | Resident in Pediatrics |
| 1993 - present | Fellow in Pediatric Critical Care |
| | Medical College of Virginia |
| | Richmond, VA |

WORK HISTORY:

My fellowship training included rotations in pediatric anesthesiology, pediatric pulmonary/bronchoscopy, transport medicine, and pediatric cardiac surgery. I worked as a locum tenens in general pediatrics during my residency and as an on-call physician in the neonatal ICU during my residency and fellowship. And covered for attending staff during the last year of my residency.

HONORS:

Dean's List: 1982 - 1986; National Dean's List, 1985; Graduated cum laude in Biology; Outstanding Senior Biology Student 1986, Athletic/Academic Excellence, 1983 - 1985; Varsity letters in cross-country and track, 1981 - 1985.

RESEARCH:

During my fellowship, I participated in a research project related to acute asthma as evaluated in pediatric ICUs.

## Resume 2—Comments

Dr. Williams' resume looks like an application form. Many application forms request personal information because that information may be needed for employment records if the candidate is hired. Applications do not give you an opportunity to present yourself in a positive manner.

- The Curriculum Vitae heading should be deleted; the document is in resume format.

- The personal information should be deleted.

- The job objective is weak; if Dr. Williams does not have a more definitive objective, that section should be deleted.

- For physicians just completing residency, omit accomplishments. What you have accomplished is well represented in the educational listing.

- Because his work history is short, Dr. Williams should consider listing his fellowship under work history.

- The format of the resume is weak—nothing stands out. A more traditional arrangement with bold subheadings leads the reader to the important sections.

- No header/footer on the second page of the document for identification.

- List honors separately to show them off.

- Personal interests would help to paint a more complete picture of Dr. Williams.

# Marvin Williams, MD

**Permanent address:**
2451 Locust Street
Galen, IL 33789
Phone: 555-365-0211
Fax: 555-365-0215
E-mail: mwmd@aol.com

**Temporary address until
July 1, 1997:**
3418 White Avenue
Richmond, VA 22345
Phone: 555-245-6781

**Job Objective:**

To join an existing practice where I can pursue my interests in working with critically ill and special needs children.

**Education:**

Tennessee University (1981 - 1986)
Jackson, TN
B.S., Biology

Tennessee University (1986 - 1990)
Jackson, TN
Doctor of Medicine

East Carolina University (1990 - 1991)
Intern in Pediatrics
Greenville, NC

East Carolina University (1991 - 1993)
Greenville, NC
Resident in Pediatrics

**Work History:**

Fellow in Pediatric Critical Care (1993 - present)
Medical College of Virginia
Richmond, VA

During fellowship, rotated in pediatric anesthesiology, pediatric pulmonary/bronchoscopy, transport medicine, and pediatric cardiac surgery.

**Work History** (cont.)

> Volunteered two nights each week to work with infants needing special care and their families.
>
> Locum Tenens in General Pediatrics
> (1992 - present)
> Dr. Helen Carey, MD
> Regional Medical Center
> Greenville, NC
>
> Work during vacations and semester breaks.
>
> On-Call Physician (1992 - 1993)
> Neo-natal ICU
> Shriner's Hospital
> Greenville, NC
>
> Worked on-call in addition to duties as a resident.

**Honors:**

> Dean's List: 1982 through 1986
> National Dean's List, 1985
> Graduated cum laude with a B.S. in Biology
> Outstanding Senior Biology Student 1986

**Personal Interests:**

> Cross-country running (when time permits). During college received Athletic/Academic Excellence Award (1983 - 1985); earned varsity letters in cross-country and track, 1981 - 1985.

**Research:**

> During fellowship, participated in a research project related to acute asthma as evaluated in pediatric ICUs.

References available on request.

Century, 11 pt.
Chronological style

# SUSAN JEAN COSTAL MD

4890 Willton Boulevard
Seattle, WA 30896

Phone: 555-465-2397
Fax: 555-465-2398

## JOB OBJECTIVE

Oncologist and oncology consultant in a large multispecialty practice

## SKILLS

Teaching
Research
Patient Care
Consulting

## WORK HISTORY

Approximately ten years experience (1988 - 1997) as oncologist in a large, multispecialty practice (46 physicians). Treated patients and consulted with other physicians in the group on oncological problems.

## EDUCATION

Grosse Pointe High School (1974 - 1977) - Valedictorian
University of Michigan (1977 - 1983) - B.S./M.D. program
William Beaumont Hospital (1983 - 1984) - Intern
William Beaumont Hospital (1984 - 1987) - Resident
Western Reserve Care System (1987 - 1988) - Cancer Fellow

## PERSONAL INTERESTS

Music

## OTHER INTERESTS

Oncology Strategy Working Group, William Beaumont Hospital, 1987
Participated in several research projects on the diagnosis and treatment of
lung cancer, 1993
Review oncology related articles for the Harvard Women's Health Letter
Speak French

## Resume 3—Comments

Dr. Costal threw this resume together too quickly. It is curt and uninteresting, and the layout looks more like an advertisement or announcement than a resume. A poorly conceived resume may be worse than none at all.

- The first line of the resume is improper. The designation of a medical degree is either MD (preferred) or M.D., but it is *always* separated from the name by a comma.

- The job objective is a description of her present work! Why is she looking for another job?

- The skills listed are not described fully enough to differentiate Dr. Costal from other physicians.

- The description of her work history is skimpy for a ten-year job.

- Omit the high school citation.

- Each university and hospital in the education section needs a location (city and state).

- Dr. Costal's interest in music and the hodgepodge of items in Other Interests needs better organization and more complete explanations.

# SUSAN JEAN COSTAL, MD

4890 Willton Boulevard
Seattle, WA 30896

Phone: 555-465-2397
Fax: 555-465-2398

## SKILLS

- Advising and consulting with other practitioners regarding oncological problems.
- Counseling patients and practitioners in dealing with terminal illnesses.
- Facilitating group dynamics and problem solving.

## WORK HISTORY

Oncologist (1987 to present)
River Forest Health Group (RFHG)
Seattle, WA

- Provide care to patients referred by other members of RFHG (46 physicians); consult with specialists in RFHG on diagnosing cancer and determining the most appropriate and effective form of treatment. (RFHG offers both medical oncology and radiation oncology treatment options.)

- Through hospital and PHO affiliations, counsel primary care physicians who are not part of the River Forest Health Group on special oncology-related problems and treatments.

- Serve as one of three managing partners in the Group; conduct problem-solving meetings, work with ancillary staff on interpersonal dynamics.

Various part-time jobs during school (1976 - 1982)

Jobs included receptionist, counselor in a camp for diabetic children, traveling companion for an elderly family member, waitress, and temporary office worker.

EDUCATION

University of Michigan (1977 - 1983)
Ann Arbor, MI
B.S./M.D. program

William Beaumont Hospital (1983 - 1984)
Detroit, MI
Intern

William Beaumont Hospital (1984 - 1987)
Detroit, MI
Resident

Western Reserve Care System (1987 - 1988)
Youngstown, OH
Cancer Fellow

LICENSES / CERTIFICATIONS

Michigan, 1983, #45802
Washington, 1987, #89896

PROFESSIONAL SOCIETIES

American Medical Association (Member; former resident representative to
the House of Delegates)
Washington State Medical Society
Oncology Strategy Working Group, William Beaumont Hospital, 1987
American Cancer Society
Washington Cancer Society

PUBLICATIONS

Co-authored numerous articles during fellowship addressing a variety of
topics; five publications in the diagnosis and treatment of lung cancer.

Serve as reviewer for oncology-related articles for the Harvard Women's
Health Letter.

## PERSONAL INTERESTS

The study and practice of group facilitation; currently enrolled in night classes in Organizational Development at the University of Seattle.

Avid opera fan with a long-term goal of visiting all the major opera houses in Europe.

References and publications list available on request. Please do not contact present employer.

Times Roman, 12 pt.
Combination style

# *J. Fernando Gonsalvo, MD*

3445 Landover Street, Apt. 15
Newark, NJ

Contact at home:
Phone: 555-342-5679
E-mail: gonsalvo@innet.com

Contact at Work:
Phone: 555-342-5679
Fax: 555-342-7987
E-mail: JFGon@aol.org

## JOB OBJECTIVE:

To obtain a position in emergency medicine in Georgia

## EDUCATION

| | |
|---|---|
| University of Texas Health Center Department of Emergency Medicine San Antonio, TX | Resident 1995 to present |
| New York Hospital-Cornell Medical Center New York, NY | Intern 1994 - 1995 |
| Wayne State U Medical School Detroit, MI | Medical Doctor 1990 - 1994 |
| Wayne State Detroit, MI | B.S., Mathmatics 1984 - 1990 |

## HONORS AND AWARDS

Wayne State University, B.S., Mathmatics, with honors
4 academic scholarship awards (undergraduate and medical school)
Outstanding Mathmatics Senior, 1990
Letters of commendation in emergency medicine (1995 and 1996)

## WORK HISTORY

Research Assistant (part-time, February 1997 to present)
University of Texas Health Center

Resume of J.F. Gonsalvo, MD, page 2

Conducting chart reviews on patients injured in automobile accidents. Principal Investigator: Dr. Randall G. Shotts.

Self-employed (part-time,1980 to 1994)
Math Tutor

During high school, college, and medical school, tutored students in math; averaged 15 hours per week during the school year and full time during summer and holiday breaks.

Letters of reference and commendations attached.

## Resume 4—Comments

At first glance, Dr. Gonsalvo's resume looks good. But the proofreading was sloppy and some inconsistencies show up.

- The telephone numbers for work and home are the same. If true, both don't need to be listed.

- He may have been a whiz in college but he still can't spell mathematics!

- The colleges attended vary from full names (New York Hospital - Cornell Medical Center) to a much shortened form (Wayne State). The full name of the institution should appear.

- Under Honors and Awards, the second line should read "Four academic scholarship awards." When a number is used as the first word of a sentence, it should be written in full.

- The city and state of each employer should be noted in the work history section.

- The attachment of references and commendations is not usually recommended. If this resume is being distributed as a mass mailing, inclusion of a few letters of reference and commendation would be acceptable.

- The page appears crowded, and the page break is awkward. Respacing the information, adding some white space, produces a much more attractive document.

# J. Fernando Gonsalvo, MD

3445 Landover Street, Apt. 15
Newark, NJ 18934

Contact at home:
Phone: 555-342-5679
E-mail: gonsalvo@internetMCI.com

Contact at Work:
Phone: 555-342-6676
Fax: 555-342-7987
E-mail: JFGon@aol.org

## JOB OBJECTIVE:

To obtain a position in emergency medicine in Georgia

## EDUCATION

| | | |
|---|---|---|
| University of Texas Health Center Department of Emergency Medicine San Antonio, TX | Resident | 1995 to present |
| New York Hospital-Cornell Medical Center New York, NY | Intern | 1994 - 1995 |
| Wayne State University Medical School Detroit, MI | Medical Doctor | 1990 - 1994 |
| Wayne State University Detroit, MI | B.S., Mathematics | 1984 - 1990 |

## HONORS AND AWARDS

Wayne State University, B.S., Mathematics, with honors
Four academic scholarship awards (undergraduate and medical school)
Outstanding Mathematics Senior, 1990
Letters of commendation in emergency medicine (1995 and 1996)

## WORK HISTORY

Research Assistant (part-time, February 1997 to present)
University of Texas Health Center
San Antonio, TX

Conducting chart reviews on patients injured in automobile accidents.
Principal Investigator: Dr. Randall G. Shotts.

Self-employed (part-time, 1980 to 1994)
Math Tutor

During high school, college, and medical school, tutored students in math; averaged 15 hours per week during the school year and full time during summer and holiday breaks.

Letters of reference and commendations attached.

Arial, 11 pt.
Chronological style

# Chris W. Wolford, MD

3535 Southern Avenue
Reno, NV 33490

Phone:      555-345-2897
Fax:        555-345-2880
E-mail:     cwolford@zyzy.com

## OBJECTIVES

To obtain a position with a major managed care organization
To continue working in utilization management

## RELATED ACCOMPLISHMENTS

Developed and implemented a utilization management program for a large medical group; the UM program was instrumental in increasing the number of major managed care contracts from one to four in three years.

Studied managed care administration and the importance of measuring both under- and overutilization of services.

Educated physicians about utilization patterns and assist in correcting inappropriate use of resources.

## EDUCATION

Harvard Medical School and Peter Bent Brigham Hospital
Boston, MA
Fellowship in Medicine/Clinical Epidemiology (August 1977 - June 1979)

Duke University Medical Center
Durham, NC
Residency in Family Medicine (July 1974 - June 1977)

Duke University Medical Center
Durham, NC
Doctor of Medicine (June 1972)

University of Texas
Austin, TX
B.A. in Microbiology (January 1967)

WORK HISTORY

Western Medical Clinic
Reno, NV
July 1990 to present

Organized a satellite office of the Las Vegas Western Medical Clinic; recruited physicians and other staff, developed the physical facility, operated as managing partner for two years. Currently, care for patients three days per week and manage the UM program for Clinic in both Las Vegas and Reno.

Western Medical Clinic
Las Vegas, NV
Department of Family Medicine
June 1985 - June 1990

Practiced family medicine in a rapidly growing clinic.

Michael Reese Hospital and Medical Center
Chicago, IL
Division of Primary Care, Department of Family Medicine
December 1979 - April 1985

Employed in a staff model HMO of approximately 60 physicians practicing family medicine.

## Resume 5—Comments

Dr. Wolford has prepared a good work-related resume. His accomplishments are well stated and his work history is clear and complete. But the impression is one of all work and no outside interests or activities.

This resume needs some highlighting—nothing stands out. By centering the subheadings and making them bold, the resume is easier to read.

The problems with the resume are easily fixed. In addition to the highlighting, personal dimensions are added in the sections marked Professional Societies and Personal Interests.

Note that Dr. Wolford did not give his office phone number *and* he stated that he did not wish to be contacted at his office. Omitting the phone number may not be sufficient to keep people from calling. If you do not wish to be contacted at your office, say so explicitly.

# Chris W. Wolford, MD

3535 Southern Avenue
Reno, NV 33490

Phone:      555-345-2897
Fax:         555-345-2880
E-mail:     cwolford@zyzy.com

## OBJECTIVES

To obtain a position with a major managed care organization
To continue working in utilization management

## RELATED ACCOMPLISHMENTS

Developed and implemented a utilization management program for a large
medical group; the UM program was instrumental in increasing the number
of major managed care contracts from one to four in three years.

Studied managed care administration and the importance of measuring both
under- and overutilization of services.

Educate physicians about utilization patterns and assist in correcting
inappropriate use of resources.

## EDUCATION

Harvard Medical School and Peter Bent Brigham Hospital
Boston, MA
Fellowship in Medicine/Clinical Epidemiology (August 1977 - June 1979)

Duke University Medical Center
Durham, NC
Residency in Family Medicine (July 1974 - June 1977)

Duke University Medical Center
Durham, NC
Doctor of Medicine (June 1972)

University of Texas
Austin, TX
B.A. in Microbiology (January 1967)

## WORK HISTORY

Western Medical Clinic
Reno, NV
July 1990 to present

- Organized a satellite office of the Las Vegas Western Medical Clinic.
- Recruited physicians and other staff.
- Developed the physical facility; operated as managing partner for two years.
- Currently, care for patients three days per week and manage the UM program for Clinic in both Las Vegas and Reno.

Western Medical Clinic
Las Vegas, NV
Department of Family Medicine
June 1985 - June 1990

Practiced family medicine in a rapidly growing clinic.

Michael Reese Hospital and Medical Center
Chicago, IL
Division of Primary Care, Department of Family Medicine
December 1979 - April 1985

Employed in a staff model HMO of approximately 60 physicians practicing family medicine.

## RELATED SPECIAL TRAINING

Managed Care Administration, two week-long seminars at the University of Michigan, June and October 1991.

Several weekend seminars offered by the American College of Physician Executives.

## LICENSES

Illinois, #56802
Nevada, #44634

## CERTIFICATIONS

American Board of Family Practice (1977, 1984, 1989, 1995)
American Board of Medical Management (1993)

## PROFESSIONAL SOCIETIES

American College of Physician Executives (Member)
American Medical Association (Member)
Nevada Medical Society (President, 1989)

## PERSONAL INTERESTS

Active in local government. Served as Neighborhood Committee Chairman, Sun Center Neighborhood, Reno, NV, from 1990 to 1994.

Las Vegas Chamber of Commerce Board of Directors, 1987 to 1989.

Lions Club, Las Vegas (1985 - 1990); Reno (1990 to present); Man of the Year in Reno, 1992.

Organized a fund-raising drive for the Lions Club charities in 1993; collected $132,000.

References available on request. Please do not contact me at the office.

Times Roman, 11 pt.
Combination style

# Chapter Three

# Distributing your resume and writing cover letters

## Distributing your resume

Usually, you will send your resume in response to a known job opening. Perhaps you are responding to an advertisement placed in a professional journal or in the local newspaper. Maybe you heard about a job from a colleague. A search firm may have contacted you and asked you to submit your resume for an opening they have listed

You may choose—or be asked—to send a resume in response to a call from a professional recruiting firm because they have heard of you and want to have your credentials in their databank.

At other times, you may choose to mass mail your resume, sending it to a list of companies or practices that have no known vacancies but that might refer you to other job sources. For example, if you are just completing your residency, have decided that you wish to begin your practice in Georgia, but have not yet located an opening, you might send your resume to the chief of staff of every hospital the American Hospital Association's directory lists in Georgia and ask for possible job leads.

If the professional organizations in your specialty maintain job banks, you will want to supply them with a copy of your resume.

Planning to attend an educational conference in the near future? Have a resume handy so that you can respond quickly to any indication of interest in you as a job candidate.

If your network of professional colleagues or classmates from medical school might be helpful in producing job leads, send them copies of your resume.

The following table lists items that you might distribute with your resume.

| If You Are: | Include This in Your Resume Package |
|---|---|
| Responding to an advertisement for a job vacancy. | • Resume.<br>• Cover letter that responds to the requirements of the job as stated in the ad. |
| Seeking an interview for a possible job that has not been advertised but that you believe or know is open. | • Resume.<br>• Cover letter that responds to the requirements of the job as you know them and how you found out about the opening. |
| Applying for an academic or research position. | • Resume.<br>• Cover letter individualized for the specific job.<br>• Publications list.<br>• Research grants and projects (either as a separate list or included in the resume). |
| Mailing many resumes to generate a list of possible jobs (mass mailing). | • Resume.<br>• Cover letter that encourages recipient to share with others.<br>• Letters of reference or list of potential references.* |
| Responding to a request from a search or professional placement firm (see notes about working with search firms below). | • Resume.<br>• Cover letter with job objective.<br>• Publications list, if requested.<br>• Research information, if requested.<br>• References, if requested. |

*Usually it is not a good idea to send reference letters or lists with your resume. However, in some circumstances, doing so may help to stimulate the recipient to contact others.

If you decide to work with a search firm, be sure the firm understands your conditions for interview. A well-stated job objective is a good beginning. Most recruiters will tell you what they would like you to include in your resume package.

It is also important to know how search firms scan your resume. Most of them look for applicants whose lifestyles are similar to those in the community where a job exists. If the community is rural, they look for someone with an affinity for small towns. They attempt to determine family preferences, as well (eg, proximity to friends and relatives, access to cultural activities). Much of what they are seeking is personal information, so expect to be asked about family and personal preferences.

Most firms are hired by the organization that has a job to fill and may be more concerned about the organization's needs than yours. Other firms can represent you and help to uncover jobs that you might not learn about. Still others are not paid full fees unless they make a placement that sticks—usually at least six months. These firms must be concerned about both the needs of the organization and your preferences.

Search firms usually conduct a screening interview by telephone, which they will arrange in advance at your convenience and which will last from 15 to 45 minutes. If the firm does not ask for such an interview, request one before you agree to an interview for placement in a job. Remember that they are looking at your resume while talking with you and trying to get a clear picture of you and your qualifications. They will have previously reviewed your resume for these qualities:

- Meaningful and explicit job descriptions.

- Frequency of job changes and progression in your career.

- Overall appearance and professionalism as shown in the resume preparation.

- Language, grammar, spelling, format, and layout of your resume and correspondence.

- Blanks, omissions, and overlaps—particularly in education and work experience.

Clearly, search firms consider the quality of the resume that you provide to be very important.

# Writing cover letters

Regardless of which methods you use to distribute your resume, the inclusion of a cover letter is a must. Even if you distribute your resume at a conference or to members of your collegial network, follow up with a personal letter to the person to whom you gave your resume. A cover letter introduces you and your resume to the employer or recruiter and establishes your interests. It can also serve to remind your network of your qualifications. Whenever possible, the letter should be tailored to the specific job and company or practice, and it should succinctly present your qualifications for the job.

## Tip

Effective cover letters are brief and to the point. Here are the essentials.

- **First paragraph:** Explain why you are writing and how you heard about the job vacancy. If you don't know whether there is a vacancy but you would like to be considered whenever there is one, indicate that you are writing because of the reputation of the company, practice, or organization.

- **Second paragraph:** State why you believe your background and experience are suited to the position. Note some of your specific experiences that can contribute to the organization. Don't repeat exactly what is in your resume (eg, don't quote the Accomplishment section directly). Create new phrases to convey your suitability for the job. This section could expand to an additional paragraph.

- **Closing paragraph:** Tell the reader of your interest in the job and request a phone or personal interview. Refer to the contact information on your resume or, if contacting you is difficult, indicate when you will make a follow-up call.

**Stop.** Three or four paragraphs, backed by the information in your resume, should be enough to set the stage for an interview.

Think of your correspondence with a prospective employer from the perspective of the reader rather than that of the writer. As the reader, you want to know how well the applicant meets the specifications of the job. How well does the applicant's background match the organization's needs? How well does the applicant meet the expectations for this position? Answer these questions for the recruiter by stating how you possess the skills the employer needs and the experience it is seeking. A cover letter is another of your sales tools and the document in which you distinguish yourself from all other potential candidates.

Here are a few general comments about cover letters:

- *Cover letters are more effective if they are addressed to a specific person.* Some advertisements will list the recruiter by name; others will not. If at all possible, try to find out the name and title of the person who will be conducting the search or the interview. Telephone to get as much information as possible and address your letter to the person by name.

- *If you are unable to obtain the name of the recruiter, do not address the letter to "Gentlemen" or "Sirs."* The use of a title such as Medical Director or Dear Sir or Madam is more appropriate (and politically correct).

- *Never handwrite a cover letter.* It may seem more personal to, you but it implies sloppiness or less than professional behavior.

- *Do not fax your cover letter or resume unless specifically asked to do so.* Faxed resumes seldom retain their original attractiveness. The same applies to e-mail. If you must send your resume as an e-mail attachment, send the files in "text only" format to facilitate conversion and use by the recipient.

- *Be concise.* Your cover letter should not exceed one page except under unusual circumstances. But don't crowd the page just to get a few more words in. Leave some white space and use bulleted phrases instead of full sentences if you need more space.

- *Remember the organization.* The first paragraph of your cover letter is introductory. The second paragraph expands on your candidacy and lists specific ways in which your background fits the job. In another paragraph you can express what you know about the firm or practice and your interest in the position. The final paragraph asks for an interview.

- *Close your cover letter with "Sincerely," "Sincerely yours," or "Yours truly."* Sign your full name, including your middle initial, unless you are well acquainted with the person to whom you are writing. In that case, your first name as a signature is acceptable.

- *The same guidelines you used for checking your resume apply to cover letters.* Check the grammar, spelling, and punctuation. When you think everything is perfect, ask someone else to check it, too. Proofread the letter several times before mailing it.

- *Use a format for your cover letter that is compatible with your resume.* The sample letters in the next section are shown in full block and modified block style. In full block style, all elements of the letter begin at the left margin. In modified block style, your address, the date of the letter, and the closing are near the right margin, and all other elements (addressee, salutation, and body) begin on the left margin. In both styles, paragraphs have a ragged right margin. The full block style is the most commonly used style in business correspondence. The sample letters also name the font used and the suggested type size. You will find additional help in formatting all your correspondence in Appendix E.

Many organizations scan resumes into a database and store them electronically. Make sure that your letters are printed on a letter-quality printer that uses simple, clear fonts—usually the same fonts used in your resume. Appendix D offers a checklist of additional suggestions for resumes and cover letters that may be scanned.

Following are sample introductory, second, and closing paragraphs from effective cover letters.

## Sample Introductory Paragraphs

Letter 1

Dear Dr. Miller:

Thank you for talking with me yesterday about the position of assistant professor at the Health Sciences Regional College. I appreciate your taking the time to describe the job to me. Your description made me realize that my ten years of training allied health personnel for the Wilson Medical Center makes me well suited for the position. As you suggested, I am enclosing my resume.

Letter 2

Dear Ms. Tenley:

I am responding to the advertisement in the March issue of the *Journal of Pediatrics* for a pediatrician to join an existing practice affiliated with a hospital network in eastern Indiana. Your network has an excellent reputation among pediatricians, and I am pleased to submit my resume for consideration.

Letter 3

Dear Dr. Wilson:

A colleague and mutual acquaintance of ours, Dr. Woodley McIntosh, told me of your organization's interest in adding an oncologist to the group. My experience in working with a large multispecialty group similar to yours is delineated in my attached resume.

Letter 4

To Whom It May Concern:

I am writing to you to seek your assistance in identifying practice opportunities in emergency medicine in your community. I will complete my residency in July 1998 and am eager to practice in the state of Georgia. I have attached my resume for your consideration.

Letter 5

Dear Mr. Davidson:

At a recent meeting between St. Patrick's Hospital PHO and representatives of the New Wave Health Plan, one of the speakers indicated that New Wave is seeking an assistant medical director to be in charge of utilization management. I believe that my experience is pertinent to that position, and I am enclosing my curriculum vitae for your deliberation.

## Sample Second Paragraph (Body of the Letter)

Letter 1

Teaching has been a part-time effort for me while conducting my medical practice. However, it has always been one of the most enjoyable activities in my professional life. Some of my teaching experiences pertinent to my understanding of the job of assistant professor include the following:

— Developed courses in nursing skills for registered nurses working in orthopedic practices.

— Assisted in the development of a cardiopulmonary resuscitation program for residents of a retirement village.

— Created an education program for families with members who are dependent on wheelchairs or orthopedic devices.

In 1994, Memorial Hospital recognized my enthusiasm for helping others to cope with their health problems by naming me Physician of the Year.

Letter 2

During my pediatric residency, which included the traditional clinical courses and rotations, I volunteered two nights each week to work with infants needing special care. One of the most exciting aspects of that work was the interaction with the families of these children and the Department of Psychiatry staff who worked with the residents in helping parents cope with the stresses of having special-care infants. In this volunteer capacity, I gained experience working with a number of individuals of various ages and socioeconomic backgrounds. With your extensive network of hospitals, I am sure there are many special care situations that might benefit from my experience.

## Letter 3

Our medical group employs 46 physicians in a variety of specialties. For over ten years I have:

- consulted with these specialists on a variety of oncological cases.

- worked closely with primary care physicians in the community who sought help in diagnosis and treatment of cancer.

- collaborated with the radiation oncologist in the practice to ascertain the best approach to treating patients.

All of these activities require not only up-to-date knowledge of oncological treatment routines and pharmacology but also a tactful, understanding, and nonthreatening approach to working with other physicians. Since your organization is considering the inclusion of an oncologist for the first time, these activities and experiences could be valuable in establishing and maintaining collegial relationships within the group.

## Letter 4

During my residency, I have thoroughly enjoyed the excitement of emergency medicine. Some of my assignments were in small to medium-sized community hospitals which regularly experience a variety of emergency cases. Georgia was my home for many years, and I would like to return to a Georgia community so that I can repay through service some of the advantages that I gained while growing up there. My academic background is strong, and you will find the recommendations from my residency mentors are outstanding.

Letter 5

When our primary care group signed its first managed care contract, we realized that utilization management was a major concern for both parties to the contract. I volunteered to learn about UM policies and procedures and devise programs or activities that would make our group attractive to our current and future managed care contracts.

— Attended two week-long seminars on managed care administration at the University of Michigan.

— Enrolled in a JCAHO seminar on utilization management.

— Developed a computer program that captures basic UM data for each of the physicians in the group and established thresholds for both over- and underutilization on several key procedures.

— Encouraged and cajoled my fellow physicians to participate in regularly scheduled discussions about our utilization patterns.

These activities demonstrate not only what I have learned about UM but also my enthusiasm for the subject.

## Sample Closing Paragraphs

Letters 1 and 2 can be concluded quite simply:

I hope this brief letter conveys my enthusiasm for the position we discussed (or advertised). I am available for an interview at your convenience and look forward to meeting with you soon.

Letter 3 requires a little more finesse since it is not clear that a job exists. The applicant might close the cover letter with:

I would be pleased to meet with you or with other members of your group to discuss how adding an oncologist to the group might be beneficial. Clearly, if the decision is positive, I would like to be considered a candidate. I can be available for an early morning or evening meeting at your convenience, and I look forward to hearing from you.

Letter 4 should give the receivers the option of forwarding your resume if they know of other opportunities that might suit your needs. The closing might say:

> If you know of any positions in emergency medicine, I would appreciate your contacting me, or you can feel free to forward my resume to other organizations that could use my services.

A closing for Letter 5 might include the need for confidentiality since the writer is currently working in the community in which the job exists. End the letter with:

> I am very interested in discussing the Assistant Medical Director position with you at your earliest convenience. I do, however, request that my interest remain confidential since I have not indicated to my partners that I am seeking a change in my position. I will call you on Tuesday to determine your interest in my qualifications.

Turn to the next section to see how these letters can work for you or, if improperly assembled, can work against you.

## Thank you letters

After you have had an interview—whether by phone or in person—send a note of appreciation. This is not just a courtesy; it also reminds the interviewer that you are serious and enthusiastic about the job for which you were interviewed. If you are not interested in the specific job, your thank you note will remind the interviewer/recruiter of your experience and background in case other, more appropriate positions become available in the near future.

During your interview, try to determine how quickly the company is planning to hire someone. If you haven't heard from them in the period of time allotted for that decision, give the interviewer a call to see where your candidacy stands. If you are no longer being considered, send a note of appreciation for the interview anyway. If you are unable to get a commitment from the interviewer about the time needed to fill the vacancy, wait two weeks before you call.

A thank you letter—one page—should be a simple statement of appreciation. Below are a few samples.

Dear Dr. Miller:

I enjoyed our interview this week regarding the position of Assistant Professor in the Health Sciences Regional College. The College's philosophy of education and the multidisciplinary approach to teaching allied health students is exciting and innovative. I would be pleased to be considered for a faculty position.

As we spoke, I was struck by the similarities between the full-fledged academic position that you described and my more informal work with our medical group's ancillary staff and with patients and their families. I look forward to hearing from you soon.

Dear Ms. Tenley:

I appreciated the opportunity to talk with you yesterday about the pediatric positions listed with your search firm. Naturally, I was disappointed that the position in Indiana was filled but gratified that other opportunities might become available soon.

As we agreed, my interest in serving families with children who require special care sets my candidacy apart from many other pediatricians who are seeking to join existing practices. Please keep my credentials in mind for other practice opportunities where my skills can be used.

Dear Dr. Wiley:

I have just learned that you sent my resume to Dr. Harmon at St. Clare's Hospital in Macon in response to his need for an emergency room physician. Thank you for that courtesy. Dr. Harmon and I are meeting next week to discuss the position. I hope that I have the opportunity to thank you in person one day.

Turn to the next section to see how these letters should be formatted.

# Letter writing exercise

## Eight important letters—before and after: An exercise

Following are five cover letters that could be used to submit a resume and three thank you letters to send as follow-ups to interviews. To help you learn to spot poorly prepared letters, each sample is presented first with some flaws in content and format—the *Before* version.

Read the *Before* letter and note the errors and problems that you spotted. Then check yourself by reading the answers and comments that follow each example to see if you caught all the boners.

Look at the improvements in the sample *After* letters. Each of the *After* letters notes the style and font used, as well as the suggested type size, and indicates whether the letter has been centered on the page or prepared in modified or full block style. The fonts used are common ones that should be available on your personal or office word processor or from any of the printing and copying shops that can help you format and print your resume.

Repeat the exercise with each of the five cover letters, and review the three thank you letters. Seeing these common mistakes will help you to develop your own—perfect—letters.

# JOHN M. WENGLEY, MD

August 15, 1997

Dr. J.F. Miller, MD
Professor, Allied Health Department
Health Sciences Regional College
1453 Arlington Place
Arlington, VA 44467

Thank you for talking with me yesterday about the position of assistant professor at the Health Sciences Regional College. I appreciate your taking the time to describe the job to me. Your description made me realize that my ten years of training allied health personnel for the Wilson Medical Center makes me well suited for the position.

Teaching has been a part-time effort for me while conducting my medical practice. However, it has always been one of the most enjoyable activities in my professional life. Some of my teaching experiences pertinent to my understanding of the job of assistant professor include the following:

    —Developed courses in nursing skills for registered nurses working in orthopedic practices.
    —Assisted in the development of a cardiopulmonary resuscitation program for residents of a retirement village.
    —Created a education program for families with members who are dependent on wheelchairs or orthopedic devices.

In 1994, Memorial Hospital recognized my enthusiasm for helping others to cope with their health problems by naming me Physician of the Year.

I hope this brief letter conveys my enthusiasm for the position we discussed. I am available for an interview at your convenience and look forward to meeting with you soon.

Sincerely,

John M. Wengley, MD

## Letter 1—Comments

- No address for Dr. Wengley. If the cover letter gets separated from his resume, it will be difficult to get in touch with him.

- No salutation. Not a friendly way to begin.

- Insufficient space for a signature.

- No indication that a resume is enclosed.

- In the third bullet phrase, *a* should be *an*.

## JOHN M. WENGLEY, MD
2861 Arizona Avenue
Washington, DC 55324

August 15, 1997

Dr. J.F. Miller, MD
Professor, Allied Health Department
Health Sciences Regional College
1453 Arlington Place
Arlington, VA 44467

Dear Dr. Miller:

Thank you for talking with me yesterday about the position of assistant professor at the Health Sciences Regional College. I appreciate your taking the time to describe the job to me. Your description made me realize that my ten years of training allied health personnel for the Wilson Medical Center makes me well suited for the position. As you suggested, I am enclosing my resume.

Teaching has been a part-time effort for me while conducting my medical practice. However, it has always been one of the most enjoyable activities in my professional life. Some of my teaching experiences pertinent to my understanding of the job of assistant professor include the following:

— Developed courses in nursing skills for registered nurses working in orthopedic practices.
— Assisted in the development of a cardiopulmonary resuscitation program for residents of a retirement village.
— Created an education program for families with members who are dependent on wheelchairs or orthopedic devices.

In 1994, Memorial Hospital recognized my enthusiasm for helping others to cope with their health problems by naming me Physician of the Year.

I hope this brief letter conveys my enthusiasm for the position we discussed. I am available for an interview at your convenience and look forward to meeting with you soon.

Sincerely,


John M. Wengley, MD

Enc: Resume

Times Roman, 10 pt.
Full block style
Text centered on page

August 15, 1997
2451 Locust Street
Galen, IL 3378

Ms. Cara Tenley
Brooks and Fellows, Inc.
1463 Stratford Place
Chicago, IL 20280

Dear Ms. Tenley:

I am responding to the advertisement in the March issue of the Journal of Pediatrics for a pediatrician to join an existing practice affiliated with a hospital network in eastern Indiana. Your hospital network has an excellent reputation among pediatricians and I am pleased to submit my resume for consideration.

During my pediatric residency, which included the traditional clinical courses and rotations, I volunteered two nights each week to work with infants needing special care. One of the most exciting aspects of that work was the interaction with the families of these children and the Department of Psychiatry staff who worked with the residents in helping parents cope with the stresses of having special-care infants. In this volunteer capacity, I gained experience working with a number of individuals of various ages and socioeconomic backgrounds. With your extensive network of hospitals, I am sure there are many special care situations that might benefit from my experience.

I hope this brief letter conveys my enthusiasm for the position advertised I am available for an interview at your convenience and look forward to meeting with you soon.

Sincerely,


Marvin W. Williams, MD




Enclosure: Resume

## Letter 2—Comments

- The font used is too busy and too fancy for a business letter.

- The font is difficult to read. Even at 14-point type size, the print is too small.

- Placement on the page is awkward. The letter would look better if the text were centered.

- Style is inconsistent. The date and address are modified block style; the closing and signature are full block.

August 15, 1997
2451 Locust Street
Galen, IL 33789

Ms. Cara Tenley
Brooks and Fellows, Inc.
1463 Stratford Place
Chicago, IL 20280

Dear Ms. Tenley:

I am responding to the advertisement in the March issue of the *Journal of Pediatrics* for a pediatrician to join an existing practice affiliated with a hospital network in eastern Indiana. Your hospital network has an excellent reputation among pediatricians and I am pleased to submit my resume for consideration.

During my pediatric residency, which included the traditional clinical courses and rotations, I volunteered two nights each week to work with infants needing special care. One of the most exciting aspects of that work was the interaction with the families of these children and the Department of Psychiatry staff who worked with the residents in helping parents cope with the stresses of having special-care infants. In this volunteer capacity, I gained experience working with a number of individuals of various ages and socioeconomic backgrounds. With your extensive network of hospitals, I am sure there are many special care situations that might benefit from my experience.

I hope this brief letter conveys my enthusiasm for the position advertised. I am available for an interview at your convenience and look forward to meeting with you soon.

Sincerely,

Marvin W. Williams, MD

Century, 12 pt.
Modified block style
Text centered on page

Enclosure: Resume

August 15, 1997
4890 Willton Boulevard
Seattle, WA 30896

Dr. Hadley W. Wilson
Metropolitan Medical Center
7834 Bay View Road
Seattle, WA 30924

Dear Dr. Wilson:

A colleague and mutual acquaintance of ours, Dr. Woodley McIntosh, told me of your organization's interest in adding an oncologist to the group. My experience in working with a large multispecialty group similar to yours is delined in my attached resume.

Our medical group employs 46 physicians in a variety of specialties. For over ten years I have:
• consulted with these specialists on a variety of oncological cases.
• working closely with primary care physicians in the community who sought help in diagnosis and treatment of cancer.
• had a good relationship with the radiation oncologist in the practice to ascertain the best approach to treating patients.

All of these activities require not only up-to-date knowledge of oncological treatment routines and pharmacology but also and tactful, understanding, and nonthreatening approach to working with other physicians. Since your organization is considering the inclusion of an oncologist for the first time, these activities and experences could be valuable in establishing and maintaining collegial relationships within the group.

I would be pleased to meet with you or with other members of your group to discuss how adding an oncologist to the group might be beneficial. Clearly, if the decision is positive, I would like to be considered a candidate. I can be available for an early morning or evening meeting at your convenience and I look forward to hearing from you.

Sincerely yours,


Susan Jean Costal, MD

Enc: Resume

## Letter 3—Comments

- The text was squeezed to get it all on one page and the result is unattractive—and it still requires two pages. Better to use two pages and space the letter attractively.

  When you find that the spacing of your letter is unattractive, you have several options. First, can you delete a few words or an unnecessary sentence? If you are using a word processor, can you reduce the font by one or two points? If neither is a good option or if neither produces sufficient space, then space the text so that the layout spills to the second page and the white space is attractively distributed.

- Misspellings or typos were not caught: *delined* for *delineated; and* for *a; experences* for *experiences.*

- The construction of the bulleted phrases is not parallel. When items are listed in a series, they should have parallel construction. See the After letter for proper construction.

- The text is right justified, making some of the spaces between words awkward.

- The style starts out as modified block, but the closing is full block style.

- Indenting the first word of a paragraph is viewed as old-fashioned business style. If it is used, it should be used consistently, which is not the case with this letter.

August 15, 1997
4890 Willton Boulevard
Seattle, WA 30896

Dr. Hadley W. Wilson
Metropolitan Medical Center
7834 Bay View Road
Seattle, WA 30924

Dear Dr. Wilson:

A colleague and mutual acquaintance of ours, Dr. Woodley McIntosh, told me of your organization's interest in adding an oncologist to the group. My experience in working with a large multispecialty group similar to yours is delineated in my attached resume.

Our medical group employs 46 physicians in a variety of specialties. For over ten years I have:
- consulted with these specialists on a variety of oncological cases.
- worked closely with primary care physicians in the community who sought help in diagnosis and treatment of cancer.
- collaborated with the radiation oncologist in the practice to ascertain the best approach to treating patients.

All of these activities require not only up-to-date knowledge of oncological treatment routines and pharmacology but also a tactful, understanding, and nonthreatening approach to working with other physicians. Since your organization is considering the inclusion of an oncologist for the first time, these activities and experiences could be valuable in establishing and maintaining collegial relationships within the group.

I would be pleased to meet with you or with other members of your group to discuss how adding an oncologist to the group might be beneficial. Clearly, if the decision is positive, I would like to be considered a candidate. I can be available for an early morning or evening meeting at your convenience and I look forward to hearing from you.

Sincerely yours,


Susan Jean Costal, MD

Enc: Resume

Courier, 12 pt.
Full block style

### J. Fernando Gonsalvo, MD
3445 Landover Street, Apt. 15
Newark, NJ 18934

Medical Director
Americus Hospital
712 Forsythe Street
Americus, GA 99256

I am writing to you to seek your assistance in identifying practice opportunitie in emergency medicine in your community. I have complete my residency in July 1998 and am eager to practice in the state of Georgia I have attached my resume for your consideration.

During my residency, I have thoroughly enjoyed the excitement of emergency medicine. Some of my assignments were in small to medium sized community hospitals which regularly experience a variety of emergency cases. Georgia was my home for many years, and I would like to return to a Georgia community so that I can repay through service some of the advantages that I gained while growing up there. My academic background is strong, and you will find the recommendations from my residency mentors are outstanding.

If you know of any positions in emergency medicine, I would appreciate your contacting me, or you can feel free to forward my resume to other organizations that could use my services.

J. Fernando Gonsalvo, MD

## Letter 4—Comments

- Dr. Gonsalvo is brief to the point of being curt. This looks suspiciously like a form letter, which should never be used as a cover letter for a resume.

- No date of initiation.

- No salutation.

- No closing.

- No line for signature.

- Right justified, which also contributes to the form letter look.

- Poorly spaced on the page.

- Spelling errors (or typos): *opportunitie* for *opportunity* or *opportunities.*

- Grammatical error: I have complete for I will complete.

- Failure to close the second sentence in the first paragraph with a period.

### J. Fernando Gonsalvo, MD
3445 Landover Street, Apt. 15
Newark, NJ 18934

August 15, 1997

Medical Director
Americus Hospital
712 Forsythe Street
Americus, GA 99256

Dear Director:

I am writing to you to seek your assistance in identifying practice opportunities in emergency medicine in your community. I will complete my residency in July 1998 and am eager to practice in the state of Georgia. I have attached my resume for your consideration.

During my residency, I have thoroughly enjoyed the excitement of emergency medicine. Some of my assignments were in small to medium-sized community hospitals which regularly experience a variety of emergency cases. Georgia was my home for many years, and I would like to return to a Georgia community so that I can repay through service some of the advantages that I gained while growing up there. My academic background is strong, and you will find the recommendations from my residency mentors are outstanding.

If you know of any positions in emergency medicine, I would appreciate your contacting me, or you can feel free to forward my resume to other organizations that could use my services.

Truly yours,


J. Fernando Gonsalvo, MD


Enclosure: Resume

Arial, 11 pt.
Full block style
Text centered on page

# Chris W. Wolford, MD
3535 Southern Avenue
Reno, NV 33490

August 15, 1997

Mr. James H. Davidson
Executive Vice President
New Wave Health Plan
One New Wave Plaza
Reno, NV 33487

Dear Mr. Davidson:

At a recent meeting between St. Patrick's Hospital PHO and representatives of the New Wave Health Plan, one of the speakers indicated that New Wave is seeking an assistant medical director to be in charge of utilization management.

I am very interested in discussing the Assistant Medical Director position with you at your earliest convenience. I do, however, request that my interest remain confidential since I have not indicated to my partners that I am seeking a change in my position. I will call you on Tuesday to determine your interest in my quatlifications.

Sincerely yours

Chris W. Wolford, MD

## Letter 5—Comments

- Dr. Wolford gives no hint of how his credentials and experience might fit the Health Plan's job, and it may not be evident to Mr. Davidson when he reads his resume. Dr. Wolford has missed a great opportunity to sell his talents.

- By misspelling *qualifications* in the last sentence, Dr. Wolford has presented a careless image.

- The letter is too curt and not well spaced.

- The format includes right justification.

- No indication of enclosed resume.

# Chris W. Wolford, MD
3535 Southern Avenue
Reno, NV 33490

August 15, 1997

Mr. James H. Davidson
Executive Vice President
New Wave Health Plan
One New Wave Plaza
Reno, NV 33487

Dear Mr. Davidson:

At a recent meeting between St. Patrick's Hospital PHO and representatives of the New Wave Health Plan, one of the speakers indicated that New Wave is seeking an assistant medical director to be in charge of utilization management. I believe that my experience is pertinent to that position, and I am enclosing my curriculum vitae for your deliberation.

When our primary care group signed its first managed care contract, we realized that utilization management was a major concern for both parties to the contract. I volunteered to learn about UM policies and procedures and devise programs or activities that would make our group attractive to our current and future managed care contracts.

—Attended two week-long seminars on managed care administration at the University of Michigan.

—Enrolled in a JCAHO seminar on utilization management.

—Developed a computer program that captures basic UM data for each of the physicians in the group and established thresholds for both over- and underutilization on several key procedures.

—Encouraged and cajoled my fellow physicians to participate in regularly scheduled discussions about our utilization patterns.

These activities demonstrate not only what I have learned about UM but also my enthusiasm for the subject.

I am very interested in discussing the Assistant Medical Director position with you at your earliest convenience. I do, however, request that my interest remain confidential since I have not indicated to my partners that I am seeking a change in my position. I will call you on Tuesday to determine your interest in my qualifications.

Sincerely yours


Chris W. Wolford, MD

Enclosure: Curriculum vitae

Times Roman, 10 pt.
Full block style

JOHN M. WENGLEY, MD

2861 Arizona Avenue

Washington, DC 55324

August 17, 1997

Dr. J.F. Miller, MD

Health Sciences Regional College

1453 Arlington Place

Arlington, VA 44467

Dear Dr. Miller:

I enjoyed our interview this week regarding the position of Assistant Professor in the Health Sciences Regional College. The College's philosophy of education and the multidisciplinary approach to teaching allied health students is exciting and innovative. I would be pleased to be considered for a faculty position.

Sincerely,

## Letter 6—Comments

- Left out Dr. Miller's title and department. In many universities it would take days to get delivered.

- Dr. Wengley missed an opportunity to remind Dr. Miller of why he is an ideal candidate for the job.

- No signature line. Perhaps Dr. Wengley thinks that on the basis of one short interview, he now has the right to sign with just his first name.

- Font style changed after the salutation. Be consistent.

- The letter is not attractively arranged on the page. It takes extra effort to space short letters properly.

# JOHN M. WENGLEY, MD
2861 Arizona Avenue
Washington, DC 55324

August 17, 1997

Dr. J.F. Miller, MD
Health Sciences Regional College
1453 Arlington Place
Arlington, VA 44467

Dear Dr. Miller:

I enjoyed our interview this week regarding the position of Assistant Professor in the Health Sciences Regional College. The College's philosophy of education and the multidisciplinary approach to teaching allied health students is exciting and innovative. I would be pleased to be considered for a faculty position.

As we spoke, I was struck by the similarities between the full-fledged academic position that you described and my more informal work with our medical group's ancillary staff and with patients and their families. I look forward to hearing from you soon.

Sincerely,

John M. Wengley, MD

Times Roman, 12 pt.
Full block style
Text centered on page

August 16, 1997
2451 Locust Street
Galen, IL 33789

Mr. Cara Tenley
Brooks and Fellows, Inc.
1463 Stratford Place
Chicago, IL 20280

Dear Ms. Tenley:

I appreciated the opportunity to talk with you yesterday about the pediatric positions listed with your search form. Naturally, I was disappointed that the position in Indiana was filled but gratified that other opportunities might become available soon.

As we agreed, my interest in serving families with children who require special care sets my candidacy apart from many other pediatrics who are seeking to join existing practices. Please keep my credentials in mind for other practice opportunities where may skills be used.

Sincerely,

Marvin W. Williams, MD

## Letter 7—Comments

- Major error in addressing Ms. Cara as Mr. in address.

- Several errors that proofreading should have caught: *form* for *firm, pediatrics* for *pediatricians, may* for *my,* and *can* omitted from the last sentence.

August 16, 1997
2451 Locust Street
Galen, IL 33789


Ms. Cara Tenley
Brooks and Fellows, Inc.
1463 Stratford Place
Chicago, IL 20280

Dear Ms. Tenley:

I appreciated the opportunity to talk with you yesterday about the pediatric positions listed with your search firm. Naturally, I was disappointed that the position in Indiana was filled but gratified that other opportunities might become available soon.

As we agreed, my interest in serving families with children who require special care sets my candidacy apart from many other pediatricians who are seeking to join existing practices. Please keep my credentials in mind for other practice opportunities where my skills can be used.

Sincerely,


Marvin W. Williams, MD


Century, 12 pt.
Modified block style
Text centered on page

### J. Fernando Gonsalvo
3445 Landover Street, Apt. 15
Newark, NJ 1893

August 30, 1997

Dr. Frank Wiley
Medical Director
Americus Hospital
712 Forsythe Street
Americus, GA 99256

Dear Dr. Wiley:

I have just learned that you sent my resume to Dr. Harmon at
St. Clare's Hospital in Macon in response to his need for an emergency
room physician. Thank you for that courtesy. Dr. Harmon and I are
meeting next week to discuss the position. I hope that I have the
opportunity to thank you in person one day.

Yours truly,


J. F. Gonsalvo MD

## Letter 8—Comments

- Dr. Gonsalvo got everything right—but put it on the page unattractively. Adding some white space at the beginning, placing the text near the center of the page, will improve the look of this letter.

### *J. Fernando Gonsalvo*
3445 Landover Street, Apt. 15
Newark, NJ 18934

August 30, 1997

Dr. Frank Wiley
Medical Director
Americus Hospital
712 Forsythe Street
Americus, GA 99256

Dear Dr. Wiley:

I have just learned that you sent my resume to Dr. Harmon at
St. Clare's Hospital in Macon in response to his need for an emergency
room physician. Thank you for that courtesy. Dr. Harmon and I are
meeting next week to discuss the position. I hope that I have the
opportunity to thank you in person one day.

Yours truly

J. F. Gonsalvo MD

Arial, 12 pt.
Full block btyle
Text centered on page

# Chapter Four

# Making improvements for the future

A resume is a dynamic document that must be periodically updated and improved. You should not need to make major revisions, but a resume that is out of date is useless.

## Improvements

Improvements grow out of what you learn about readers' reactions. Be wise and search out information or reactions that can make revisions of your resume even better.

If you gave copies of your resume to your professional network, ask them directly for opinions about your resume. Check on length—did it strike them as too long, too short, or about right? Were there sections that they thought were particularly well prepared? Were any descriptions unclear? What did they notice first? Mull over their comments and use them carefully. You shouldn't make adjustments just because you obtained feedback from one person. But if several readers reacted in the same way, changes may be appropriate.

Try to recall your interview. What elements caught the interviewer's eye? Were any questions asked that implied the interviewer did not understand your job descriptions? Did he or she ask questions that were clearly answered on the resume? Doing so is a sign that important elements of the resume did not stand out and need to be rearranged. Did the interviewer ask for information that was not part of your resume but that you might wish to add—excluding personal information, of course?

These impressions will be clear in your mind immediately following your interview. Take notes on the changes you want to make—and make them before the next resume goes into the mail.

# For the future

Keep your resume current. Just as you do with other personal documents (wills, insurance, investment strategies), check it annually and revise it as needed. You will be surprised at the number of small items that need to be refreshed. An up-to-date resume is good to have on hand for the following occasions:

- You are asked to present a paper or a speech at a conference and the sponsors ask for a one-page recap of your background. Just pull appropriate excerpts from your resume.

- You are asked to run for office in a professional society or local organization.

- You need to look up dates of employment or employer addresses for credentialing forms, applications for PHOs, or home mortgages.

- You decide that the job market looks good again or you hear about another perfect job.

A well-written, attractively presented resume is a personal asset that enhances your professional life. Keep it active.

# Action verbs

As you write your accomplishments, skills achieved, and job history, choose from among these action verbs to give life to your resume.

| | | | |
|---|---|---|---|
| accelerated | augmented | consolidated | directed |
| accomplished | authored | constructed | discovered |
| achieved | ———————— | consulted | dispatched |
| acquired | balanced | contacted | distributed |
| acted | billed | contracted | documented |
| acted as | bought | contributed | drafted |
| active in | broadened | controlled | ———————— |
| adapted | built | converted | earned |
| addressed | ———————— | coordinated | edited |
| administered | carried out | corrected | effected |
| advised | centralized | corresponded | eliminated |
| allocated | chaired | counseled | employed |
| analyzed | channeled | created | enacted |
| applied | charted | cultivated | enforced |
| appointed | clarified | cut | engineered |
| approved | coached | ———————— | established |
| arbitrated | collaborated | decreased | evaluated |
| arranged | collected | defined | examined |
| articulated | communicated | delegated | executed |
| assembled | compiled | delivered | exercised |
| assessed | completed | demonstrated | expanded |
| assimilated | composed | designated | expedited |
| assisted | computed | designed | extracted |
| assumed | computerized | detected | ———————— |
| responsibility | conceived | determined | facilitated |
| assured | conceptualized | developed | financed |
| attained | condensed | devised | followed up |
| audited | conducted | diagnosed | forecasted |

formulated

forwarded

founded

functioned as

—————————

gathered

generated

guided

—————————

handled

hired

—————————

identified

implemented

improved

improvised

increased

influenced

initiated

inspected

inspired

installed

instigated

instituted

instructed

insured

integrated

interfaced

interpreted

interviewed

introduced

invented

investigated

—————————

launched

lectured

led

liaised

located

maintained

managed

marketed

mediated

met with

mobilized

modified

monitored

motivated

—————————

negotiated

—————————

obtained

operated

optimized

orchestrated

ordered

organized

originated

oversaw

—————————

painted

participated

performed

persuaded

pinpointed

pioneered

planned

prepared

presented

printed

processed

procured

produced

programmed

projected

promoted

proofread

proposed

proved

provided

published

purchased

—————————

recommended

reconciled

recorded

recruited

redesigned

reduced

referred

regulated

reorganized

repaired

reported

represented

researched

resolved

restored

reviewed

revised

revitalized

—————————

saved

scheduled

screened

secured

selected

served as

set up

sold

solved

specified

sponsored

staffed

stimulated

strengthened

structured

studied

suggested

summarized

supervised

supplied

surveyed

systematized

—————————

tabulated

tailored

taught

tested

trained

translated

typed

—————————

undertook

unified

upgraded

—————————

verified

—————————

won

wrote

# Sample references list

To be provided only when requested or taken with you to an interview.

Mr. Sol Gottlieb, President          Phone: 555-134-8910
Memorial Hospital Corporation
1432 East-West Highway
Sarasota, FL 81809
(Mr. Gottlieb is the CEO at my present location; knows my management capabilities)

Ms. Sally Gillen          Phone: 555-891-3456
145 North Ocala Street
Sarasota, FL 81810
(Ms. Gillen is a member of the Board of Directors at Memorial Hospital; we worked on the reorganization project together)

Sr. Mary Clare Wilson, President          Phone: 555-345-1010
St. Anthony's Hospital
1456 Calle Sin Nombre
Albuquerque, NM 87511
(Sister Mary Clare was my administrative supervisor when I worked at St. Anthony's)

Dr. William K. Smith, MD          Phone: 555-345-9898
Metropolitan Health Clinic
1485 Washington Street
Albuquerque, NM 87514
(Dr. Smith was chief of the medical staff at St. Anthony's; knows my clinical skills well)

Mr. Roland Bigwell, CPA                    Phone: 555-245-9067
Bigwell and Bigwell
4523 Tampico Street
Sarasota, FL 18111
(Mr. Bigwell was the financial auditor and advisor for my medical
practice; assisted in the arrangements for the expansion of the
practice)

Dr. Keith Leeshur, MD                      Phone: 555-345-8934
Coventry Clinic
22678 Old South Road
Tampa, FL 99024
(Dr. Leeshur was my mentor and director of my residency program;
consults with my practice on special cases)

# Listing your publications

If you are preparing a list of publications or editing a list that already exists, here are some easy rules to follow. Assume that the person preparing the publications list is George F. Johnson, MD.

## Articles

Begin with the title of the article, listed in double quotation marks and followed by a period. The publication in which the article appears is cited in italics, followed by a comma, the date, a comma, and the page numbers of the article. (If you do not have an italic font, underline the name of the publication.) If you authored the following articles alone, here is how you might list them. If you are the sole author of each publication that you list, there is no need to list your name as author for each publication.

"Analysis of Strategies to Decrease Postanesthesia Care Unit Costs." *Journal of Anesthesia,* March 1989, pp. 24 - 29.

"The Effects of Utilization Review on Hospital Use and Expenditures." *Medical Care Review,* Fall 1990, pp. 42 - 56.

If you coauthored the article with someone else, list the articles with authors in alphabetical order.

> Whippet, Carol, et al. "The Effects of Utilization Review on Hospital Use and Expenditures." *Medical Care Review,* Fall 1990, pp. 42 - 56.
>
> Johnson, George F., and John A. Wickley. "Analysis of Strategies to Decrease Postanesthesia Care Unit Costs." *Journal of Anesthesia,* March 1989, pp. 24 - 29.
>
> Johnson, George F., Sarah Stearns, and Gary Yell. "Analysis of Strategies to Decrease Postanesthesia Care Unit Costs." *Journal of Anesthesia,* March 1989, pp. 24 - 29.

The third publication in the above list might be noted as follows if Stearns was the senior or lead author.

> Stearns, Sarah, Gary Yell, and George F. Johnson. "Analysis of Strategies to Decrease Postanesthesia Care Unit Costs." *Journal of Anesthesia,* March 1989, pp. 24 - 29.

## Book chapter

Titles of chapters or parts of a book appear in double quotes, followed by "In" in normal type and the title of the book in italics. The editor(s)' name follows the title after a comma. Page numbers are optional.

> Johnson, George F. "Postanaesthesia Care." In *Theories and Methodologies of Postoperative Medicine,* edited by William C. Harrington. Pp. 332 - 365. New Jersey: Tiger Press, 1989.

## Books

If you have published a book, the title is listed in italics, followed by a period. The location of the publisher and the publisher's name follow, separated by a colon. After the publisher's name, there is a comma and the date of publication, followed by a period.

*Ambulatory Care Management.* New York: Delmar, Inc., 1993.

*Health Care in the U.S.—Equitable for Whom?* Beverly Hills, CA: Sage Publications, 1988.

If you were coauthor of a book, list the authors in alphabetical order or, if one of the authors is a senior or lead author, list his or her name first.

Johnson, George F., Austin Ross, and Stephen Williams. *Ambulatory Care Management.* New York: Delmar, Inc., 1993.

Aday, L., and George F. Johnson. *Health Care in the U.S.— Equitable for Whom?* Beverly Hills, CA: Sage.

## Compiling the list

After you have collected all the information you need for your publications list, place everything in reverse chronological order. In a resume, there are several options for listing your publications:

- A list of publications in which you were the sole author with a separate list of coauthored publications.
- All publications in a single list.
- Books in one list and articles in a separate list.

Choose the style that presents your work in the best light. If all the publications used as examples above constituted your publications list, the publications list that includes both authored and coauthored works would look like this:

## Publications

Aday, L., and George F. Johnson. *Health Care in the U.S.—Equitable for Whom?* Beverly Hills, CA: Sage Publications, 1988.

Johnson, George F. "Postanaesthesia Care." In *Theories and Methodologies of Postoperative Medicine,* edited by William C. Harrington. Pp. 332-365. New Jersey: Tiger Press, 1989.

_____. "The Effects of Utilization Review on Hospital Use and Expenditures." *Medical Care Review,* Fall 1990, pp. 42 - 56.

_____, Austin Ross, and Stephen Williams. *Ambulatory Care Management.* New York: Delmar, Inc., 1993.

_____, Sarah Stearns, and Gary Yell. "Analysis of Strategies to Decrease Postanesthesia Care Unit Costs." *Journal of Anesthesia,* March 1989, pp. 24 - 29.

Whippet, Carol, et al. "The Effects of Utilization Review on Hospital Use and Expenditures." *Medical Care Review,* Fall 1990, pp. 42 - 56.

*Note:* The blank lines that introduce the above entries indicate that the author for those items is the same as in the preceding entry.

If you choose to make two lists, list the appropriate publications cited in the two categories. A sample of a publications list with the books and articles listed separately would look like this:

## Books Published

Aday, L., and George F. Johnson. *Health Care in the U.S.— Equitable for Whom?* Beverly Hills, CA: Sage Publications, 1988.

Johnson, George F., Austin Ross, and Stephen Williams. *Ambulatory Care Management.* New York: Delmar, Inc., 1993.

## Articles Published

Johnson, George F. "Postanaesthesia Care." In *Theories and Methodologies of Postoperative Medicine,* edited by William C. Harrington. Pp. 332-365. New Jersey: Tiger Press, 1989.

_____. "The Effects of Utilization Review on Hospital Use and Expenditures." *Medical Care Review,* Fall 1990, pp. 42 - 56.

_____, Sarah Stearns, and Gary Yell. "Analysis of Strategies to Decrease Postanesthesia Care Unit Costs." *Journal of Anesthesia,* March 1989, pp. 24 - 29.

Whippet, Carol, et al. "The Effects of Utilization Review on Hospital Use and Expenditures." *Medical Care Review,* Fall 1990, pp. 42 - 56.

# Evaluation checklist

## Check the content

Check off each of the following items to indicate that you have handled them appropriately.

- ☐ Does your full name appear at the top of the page, set off in a large font or boldface type?
- ☐ Is your full address with zip code, telephone and fax numbers with area code, and full e-mail address listed?
- ☐ Have you made sure that the telephone number listed is answered during regular business hours by a person or an answering machine or appropriate calling times are cited?
- ☐ Is your name at the top or bottom of each subsequent page?
- ☐ Did you highlight your accomplishments that are relevant experience to your employment objectives?
- ☐ Does your work history include your title, name of firm, city and state of firm, and dates of employment for each job listed?
- ☐ Are any of your job descriptions more than six lines in length?
- ☐ Have you excluded any information related to sex, age, race, marital status, or any other unnecessary personal information?
- ☐ Have you excluded salary history?
- ☐ Are your educational degrees earned listed in reverse chronological order?
- ☐ Are the sentences and phrases used short and concise?
- ☐ Have you eliminated any unnecessary repetition of words or phrases?

☐ Does the narrative use active verbs wherever possible?

☐ Did you use present tense for the description of your current job and past tense for descriptions of previous jobs?

## Review the format, design, and style

Conduct—or have someone else conduct for you—a visual examination of your printed resume. Use the following items to assist you in your evaluation.

☐ Headings and indenting are used to make categories clear and reading easy.

☐ The typestyle is conservative and easy-to-read, and no more than two different typestyles have been used.

☐ Boldface is used sparingly.

☐ Right margins are ragged, not right justified. (Justifying the right margin leaves unsightly gaps in the text.)

☐ Blank lines and generous margins are used to avoid a crowded appearance.

☐ A consistent number of lines separate items.

☐ The resume is printed on quality bond paper in white or off-white (ecru, ivory, beige, etc.).

☐ The printing is high quality (24-pin letter quality, ink jet, or laser printer).

☐ The resume is printed on one side only.

☐ The resume is not photocopied or stapled.

☐ Underlining and italics are used sparingly.

☐ Like items, such as company names, job titles, and dates, are formatted consistently.

☐ Commas are used liberally in the interest of clarity.

☐ Text has been checked and rechecked to eliminate typographical errors.

☐ A period ends every complete sentence.

☐ No exclamation points are used.

- [ ] There is consistent use of capitalization, boldfacing, and punctuation.

- [ ] There are no spelling errors.

- [ ] State names are abbreviated correctly; all are two letters as designated by the US Postal Service, and the letters are not separated by periods.

## Double check for scanning

If you think your resume will be scanned, use the following checklist in addition to the one above, even though some of the items are repeated.

- [ ] Used 8$^1$/2-x-11-inch white paper.

- [ ] Placed your name at the top of the page on its own line.

- [ ] Used standard address format below your name.

- [ ] Listed each phone number on its own line.

- [ ] Included a keyword section as well as used keywords in other parts of the resume.

- [ ] Used keywords in a sequence that complements the order of the sections.

- [ ] Used a common, sans serif typeface such as Helvetica or Arial.

- [ ] Used a font size between 10 and 14 points.

- [ ] Used boldface only as long as the letters do not touch each other.

- [ ] Used left justified and ragged right text.

- [ ] Used horizontal and vertical lines sparingly, and when you did, left a quarter-inch of white space around them.

- [ ] Used sparingly or not at all: tabs, hard returns, parentheses, brackets, etc.

- [ ] Did not use italics, script, and underlined passages.

- [ ] Did not use two-column formats.

- [ ] Did not condense spacing between letters.

- [ ] Used a 24-pin letter quality, ink jet, or laser printer.

- [ ] Did not staple or fold your resume.

# Letter organization

On the following pages, you will find two completely annotated business letters. The first has been formatted in full block style and includes a letterhead. The second is formatted in modified block style and omits a letterhead.

# JONATHAN H. HARRIS
4905 Massachusetts Avenue
Washington, DC 33467

*Leave two lines white space below address*    *Your return address: spell out in full*

August 18, 1998

*Leave one line white space below date; no abbreviations in the address.*

Ms. Jennifer Colter
Recruiting Manager
New Wave Health Plan
146 Central Avenue
Springfield, IL 89367

*Salutation begins one line below address. Always use Mr., Ms., or Dr., with surname followed by a colon.*

Dear Ms. Colter:

In a cover letter, the first paragraph should include the position sought, why you are the best candidate, and reference to the name and date of the publication where the ad appeared or reference to the person who notified you of the opportunity.

The second paragraph states what you can contribute to the organization or practice that has the job opportunity and your specific experiences relating to the requirements as you understand them.

A third paragraph, if needed, provides an opportunity to express eagerness to work for the employer and shows a specific knowledge of the organization or practice.

To close, the final paragraph should request an interview either by telephone or in person. Include your phone number and when you can be reached, or say when you will make a follow-up call.

Sincerely,

*Leave one line white space before the closing and four lines before your signature. Type your full name and sign above your name in black ink.*

Jonathan H. Harris, MD

*Place the enclosure line three to five spaces below the closing.*

Enclosure: Resume

4905 Massachusetts Avenue
Washington, DC 33467

*Leave two lines white space below address*

August 18, 1998

*Leave one line white space below date; no abbreviations in the address*

Ms. Jennifer Colter
Recruiting Manager
New Wave Health Plan
146 Central Avenue
Springfield, IL 89367

*Salutation begins after one line of white space below address. Always use Mr., Ms., or Dr., with surname followed by a colon.*

Dear Ms. Colter:

In a cover letter, the first paragraph should include the position sought, why you are the best candidate, and reference to the name and date of the publication where the ad appeared or reference to the person who notified you of the opportunity.

The second paragraph states what you can contribute to the organization or practice that has the job opportunity and your specific experiences relating to the requirements as you understand them.

A third paragraph, if needed, provides an opportunity to express eagerness to work for the employer and shows a specific knowledge of the organization or practice.

To close, the final paragraph should request an interview either by telephone or in person. Include your phone number and when you can be reached, or say when you will make a follow-up call.

*Leave one line white space before the closing and four lines before your signature. Type your full name and sign above your name in black ink.*

Sincerely,

Jonathan H. Harris, MD

*Place the enclosure line three to five spaces below the closing.*

Enclosure: Resume

*Note: The address at the top of the letter, closing, signature, and enclosure lines should be aligned.*

# Bibliography

## Cover letters and resumes

Farr, J. Michael. *The Quick Resume and Cover Letter Book.* Indianapolis, Ind.: JIST Works, Inc., 1994.

Godin, Seth. *Point and Click Jobfinder.* Chicago: Dearborn Trade Publishing, 1996. Includes an America Online floppy disk and certificate for online time.

Gonyea, James C., and Wayne M. Gonyea. *Electronic Resumes: A Complete Guide to Putting Your Resume Online.* New York: McGraw-Hill, 1995.

Ireland, Susan. *The Complete Idiot's Guide to the Perfect Resume.* New York: Simon & Schuster, Macmillan Co., 1997.

Kennedy, Joyce Lain. *Cover Letters for Dummies.* Foster City, Calif.: IDG Books Worldwide, Inc., 1996.

Provenzano, Steven. *Top Secret: Resumes and Cover Letters.* Chicago: Dearborn Trade Publishing, 1995. Paperback and CD-ROM.

## Practice management, residency information

Beall, Douglas P. "New Guidelines for Resident Contracts" (in "Code Blue," news for resident physicians from the American Medical Association), *Resident & Staff Physician,* August 1996, pp. 48–49.

Cejka, Sue. "When a $155,000 Offer Is Really $134,000 in Disguise," *Medical Economics* 74, no. 14 (July 14, 1997), pp. 162–63.

Double, Donald L. *The Physician in Transition: Managing the Job Interview.* Chicago: American Medical Association, 1997.

*Evaluating and Negotiating Compensation Arrangements: Understanding the Process and Ensuring Your Future.* Chicago: American Medical Association, forthcoming.

FREIDA online. AMA Fellowship & Residence Electronic Interactive Database Access System. Chicago: American Medical Association, annual. www.ama-assn.org

*Graduate Medical Education Directory.* Chicago: American Medical Association, annual.

## Grammar, style, and writing

*Associated Press Stylebook and Libel Manual,* 6th trade edition. Reading, Mass.: Addison-Wesley, 1996.

*The Chicago Manual of Style,* 14th edition. Chicago: University of Chicago Press, 1993.

Harnack, Andrew, and Gene Kleppinger. "Beyond the MLA Handbook: Documenting Electronic Sources on the Internet." http://www.falcon.eku.edu/honors/beyond-mla/

Strunk, William, Jr., and E. B. White. *Elements of Style.* Needham Heights, MA: Allyn & Bacon, Inc., 1995.

## Career paths

*Assessing Your Career Options.* Chicago: American Medical Association, forthcoming.

*Leaving the Bedside: The Search for a Nonclinical Medical Career.* Chicago: American Medical Association, 1996.

# It's your career.
# If you're making a change,
# we can help.

If you need concise, ready-to-use information that really addresses your unique career needs and perspectives, look to the American Medical Association (AMA) Career Management and Development books. They offer the guidance you need to make your career in medicine as satisfying and rewarding as possible.

*Assessing Your Career Options, The Physician's Resume and Cover Letter Workbook, Managing the Job Interview, Evaluating and Negotiating Compensation Arrangements, Leaving the Bedside,* and *Closing Your Practice* were designed to be easy to use and quick to read, with lots of helpful forms for organizing your thoughts and evaluating your professional needs. Choose the specific books you need to help polish your resume or curriculum vitae, sharpen your interviewing or negotiation skills, and chart your options for securing a successful future.

# Order now.
# Call the AMA at
# 800 621-8335.

Major credit cards accepted. Shipping and handling charges and state taxes where applicable.

**Leaving the Bedside,
Revised Edition**
Order #: OP392096AIA
AMA member price: $25.95
Nonmember price: $32.95

**Managing the Job Interview**
Order #: OP206297AIA
AMA member price: $14.95
Nonmember price: $19.95

**The Physician's Resume and
Cover Letter Workbook**
Order #: OP206497AIA
AMA member price: $19.95
Nonmember price: $27.95

**Closing Your Practice**
Order #: OP381697AIA
AMA member price: $16.95
Nonmember price: $27.95

**Assessing Your Career Options**
Order #: OP206397AIA
AMA member price: $24.95
Nonmember price: $32.95

**Evaluating and Negotiating
Compensation Arrangements**
Order #: OP206597AIA
AMA member price: $29.95
Nonmember price: $39.95

## American Medical Association
Physicians dedicated to the health of America

# Nikolai Dante

## The Romanov Dynasty

NIKOLAI DANTE CREATED BY

**ROBBIE MORRISON AND SIMON FRASER**

# NIKOLAI DANTE

Script: Robbie Morrison

Art: Simon Fraser

Colors: Simon Fraser, Alison Kirkpatrick

Letters: Annie Parkhouse

Originally published in *2000 AD* Progs 1035-1041

In the Year of the Tsar 2666 AD, Imperial Russia once again entered a time of troubles. The rule of Vladimir the Conqueror, Tsar of All the Russias, had been unopposed for centuries. Now it was being challenged by the House of Romanov, the most powerful Imperial Dynasty beside the Tsar's own.

Warfare on such a scale had not been contemplated since the Last Revolution, from which the Mafiya Clans rose to power. On the ashes of that conflict they founded a new Empire based upon the underworld principles of the ancient Vorovskoi Mir - The Thieves' World.

In such a world a single man could rise to prominence if he was a fool and an adventurer, a gambling man whose only stake was his life. Of course, this could only happen if he survived long enough and didn't get his throat slit in the boudoir of some Lady of dubious morals first...

SCRIPT
ROBBIE MORRISON

ART
SIMON FRASER

LETTERS
ANNIE PARKHOUSE